Math and Nonfiction
Grades K–2

Math and Nonfiction

Grades K–2

Jamee Petersen

Introduction by

Marilyn Burns

Math Solutions Publications
Sausalito, CA

Math Solutions Publications
A division of
Marilyn Burns Education Associates
150 Gate 5 Road, Suite 101
Sausalito, CA 94965
www.mathsolutions.com

Library of Congress Cataloging-in-Publication Data

Petersen, Jamee.
  Math and nonfiction. Grades K–2 / Jamee Petersen.
    p. cm.
  Includes bibliographical references and index.
   ISBN 0-941355-61-6 (alk. paper)
  1. Mathematics—Study and teaching (Early childhood) 2. Children's literature in mathematics education. I. Title.
  QA135.6P47 2004
   372.7—dc22

2004018525

ISBN-13: 978-0-941355-61-2
ISBN-10: 0-941355-61-6

Editor: Toby Gordon
Production: Melissa L. Inglis
Cover and interior design: Catherine Hawkes/Cat and Mouse
Composition: Interactive Composition Corporation

Printed in the United States of America on acid-free paper
08 07   ML   3 4 5

A Message from Marilyn Burns

We at Math Solutions Professional Development believe that teaching math well calls for increasing our understanding of the math we teach, seeking deeper insights into how children learn mathematics, and refining our lessons to best promote students' learning.

Math Solutions Publications shares classroom-tested lessons and teaching expertise from our faculty of Math Solutions Inservice instructors as well as from other respected math educators. Our publications are part of the nationwide effort we've made since 1984 that now includes

- more than five hundred face-to-face inservice programs each year for teachers and administrators in districts across the country;
- annually publishing professional development books, now totaling more than fifty titles and spanning the teaching of all math topics in kindergarten through grade 8;
- four series of videotapes for teachers, plus a videotape for parents, that show math lessons taught in actual classrooms;
- on-site visits to schools to help refine teaching strategies and assess student learning; and
- free online support, including grade-level lessons, book reviews, inservice information, and district feedback, all in our quarterly *Math Solutions Online Newsletter*.

For information about all of the products and services we have available, please visit our website at *www.mathsolutions.com*. You can also contact us to discuss math professional development needs by calling (800) 868-9092 or by sending an email to *info@mathsolutions.com*.

We're always eager for your feedback and interested in learning about your particular needs. We look forward to hearing from you.

Math Solutions®
PUBLICATIONS

To Blanche, Blake, and all in between.

Contents

Acknowledgments

Thanks to the following fabulous teachers from Forest Hills Elementary School in Eden Prairie, Minnesota, who allowed me to teach these lessons in their classrooms: Stephanie Beach, Kristin Cayo, Bonnie Holman, Shana Jensen, Kim Jessen, Bobbi Miest.

Thank you to my principal, Connie Hytjan, and thanks to Liz Stamson, who helped review the manuscript.

And to the students of Forest Hills . . . thank you.

Introduction

For months before publishing this resource of classroom-tested lessons, I was surrounded by children's books. They were stacked practically up to my ears on my desk and additional piles were all around on the floor. It took some fancy shuffling at times to make space for other things that needed my attention. But I never complained. I love children's books and it was pure pleasure to be immersed in reading them and then teaching, writing, revising, and editing lessons that use them as springboards for teaching children mathematics.

This book is one in our new Math Solutions Publications series for teaching mathematics using children's literature, and I'm pleased to present the complete series:

Math and Literature, Grades K–1
Math and Literature, Grades 2–3
Math and Literature, Grades 4–6, Second Edition
Math and Literature, Grades 6–8
Math and Nonfiction, Grades K–2
Math and Nonfiction, Grades 3–5

More than ten years ago we published my book *Math and Literature (K–3)*. My premise for that book was that children's books can be effective vehicles for motivating children to think and reason mathematically. I searched for books that I knew would stimulate children's imaginations and that also could be used to teach important math concepts and skills.

After that first book's publication, my colleague Stephanie Sheffield began sending me the titles of children's books she had discovered and descriptions of the lessons she had taught based on them. Three years after publishing my book, we published Stephanie's *Math and*

Literature (K–3), Book Two. And the following year we published Rusty Bresser's *Math and Literature (Grades 4–6)*, a companion to the existing books.

Over the years, some of the children's books we initially included in our resources have, sadly, gone out of print. However, other wonderful titles have emerged. For this new series, we did a thorough review of our three original resources. Stephanie and I collaborated on substantially revising our two K–3 books and reorganizing them into two different books, one for grades K–1 and the other for grades 2–3. Rusty produced a second edition of his book for grades 4–6.

In response to the feedback we received from teachers, we became interested in creating a book that would offer lessons based on children's books for middle school students, and we were fortunate enough to find two wonderful teachers, Jennifer M. Bay-Williams and Sherri L. Martinie, to collaborate on this project. I'm pleased to present their book, *Math and Literature, Grades 6–8*.

The two books that round out our series use children's nonfiction as springboards for lessons. Jamee Petersen created *Math and Nonfiction, Grades K–2*, and Stephanie Sheffield built on her experience with the Math and Literature books to team with her colleague Kathleen Gallagher to write *Math and Nonfiction, Grades 3–5*. Hearing nonfiction books read aloud to them requires children to listen in a different way than usual. With nonfiction, students listen to the facts presented and assimilate that information into what they already know about that particular subject. And rather than reading from cover to cover as with fiction, it sometimes makes more sense to read only a small portion of a nonfiction book and investigate the subject matter presented in that portion. The authors of these Math and Nonfiction books are sensitive to the demands of nonfiction and how to present new information in order to make it accessible to children.

We're still fond of the lessons that were based on children's books that are now out of print, and we know that through libraries, the Internet, and used bookstores, teachers have access to some of those books. Therefore, we've made all of the older lessons that are not included in the new series of books available online at *www.mathsolutions.com*. Please visit our Web site for those lessons and for additional support for teaching math.

I'm pleased and proud to present these new books. It was a joy to work on them, and I'm convinced that you and your students will benefit from the lessons we offer.

MARILYN BURNS
2004

Before and After

Jan Thornhill's *Before and After* (1997) addresses the concept of elapsed time. The book shows before and after pictures of special places all over the world, from a coral reef in the Indo-Pacific to the edge of a forest in Australia to a city schoolyard. Beginning with short increments of time—a few seconds, one minute, one hour—and extending to longer periods—one day, one month, one year—the book demonstrates how time changes environments.

The two lessons described here are suitable for first and second graders. In the first lesson, after a short game to help the students experience what a few seconds and one minute feel like, the children make drawings to represent particular increments of elapsed time. In the second lesson, the students study how ice cubes change after one minute, five minutes, and one hour, and record their observations.

MATERIALS

First Lesson

stopwatch or a watch with a second hand

Second Lesson

small cooler with ice cubes, 1 ice cube per
   student

clear plastic 8- to 10-ounce drinking glasses,
   1 per student

*B*efore and After shows seven environments before and after a specified amount of time has passed. The book's introduction encourages students to find all of the animals in the first picture, then examine the second picture to figure out how things have changed. The border of each illustration shows pictures of all of the animals in the environment and gives their names.

The Nature Notes section in the back of the book provides details about the changes in each environment. It's especially useful for clarifying changes that take place over longer periods of time—a day in a meadow or a month in a rain forest.

The First Lesson

The first and second graders gathered on the rug to hear me read the book aloud. They were enthralled by the detailed pictures and enjoyed looking for what changed between the two settings. As we studied the savannah, the students made many observations.

"The animals are all running now," started Nick, referring to the "after a minute" page.

"I think the lion made them all run," said Jessica. She requested that I turn back to the "before" picture of the savannah and continued, "Before he was sitting really quiet up there hiding in the grass and now the lion is down there chasing the animals out of the water." I turned back to the "after a minute" page so that everyone could see what Jessica described. As other students shared, I flipped back and forth between the "before" and "after a minute" pages.

William offered, "Yeah, the flamingos, zebras, giraffes, and all those other animals were drinking water from the little lake before. And then after a minute they are running because they are scared."

"The leopard woke up after a minute. He was taking a nap before," Miriam noted.

"I noticed the birds flying in the first picture are far away because they look like the letter V," Johnny said, drawing a V in the air with his finger. "And then after a minute passed they flied up close. I think they're vultures."

Next, I explained to students the quiet game we were about to play. "The game is called *Wiggly Wobbly*," I said. I showed the children the stopwatch and explained its purpose and how it worked. Hanging it around my neck, I asked students to stand quietly.

I explained, "In this game you are going to feel how long a few seconds are and how long one minute is. When I say 'wiggle,' move the top of your body but pretend that your feet have grown roots and cannot move. You can move your head, shoulders, arms, and hips," I said, demonstrating by moving. "You can bend your knees and elbows, but you just can't move your feet. When I say 'wobble,' stop moving." I stopped my own movements. "So the signal to start is 'wiggle' and the signal to stop is 'wobble.'"

The children immediately began testing out their moves. Because they were doing so calmly, I gave them a few moments to experiment.

I then asked for their attention. When they were quiet and still, I said, "OK, ready? Wiggle!" Using the stopwatch, I timed five seconds and then said, "Wobble!" All but a few children immediately became still. Once they had all stopped wiggling, I said, "That time, just a few seconds passed. Let's try it again and I'll change the amount of time I give you. Ready? Wiggle!" I timed one minute, then said, "Wobble!" This time, all the children were immediately quiet. I repeated the game once more, timing five seconds again. The expressions on the children's faces and their giggles told me that they were having a great time.

After the students settled down again I asked, "Which time felt longer—a few seconds or a minute?"

"A minute," they trumpeted.

"OK, so now that you know how long a minute feels, let's think about what sorts of things you can do in one minute." I wrote on the board: *after one minute.*

"Wash your hands," Muriel began.

"Write my name in cursive," Harley said proudly.

"Count to . . . ," Catherine contemplated, then said, "a hundred."

"Toast a bagel because I stand there and watch the toaster and it seems like about a minute," Brock described.

As the students offered their ideas, I recorded them on the board under the heading I had written. Other suggestions included "put on my coat, hat, and mittens," "run around the gym twice," "make a touchdown," "pour a glass of juice," "open a letter," "tie my shoes," "make my bed," "sharpen my pencil," and "fall asleep." We talked about these tasks and the idea that, while some people might take more or less time to do each task, each one could be done in a minute.

I then said, "A couple of times I said 'wobble' after just a few seconds had elapsed." (Throughout the lesson I used the words *elapsed* and *passed* interchangeably so the students could become comfortable with the new terminology.) "What do you think I mean by 'a few' seconds?"

"Maybe ten," Mark said.

"Two or three?" Hannah questioned.

"A few is supposed to mean a little, except when it's my mom and she is on the phone, then a few minutes means a long time," Karina said in an exasperated tone.

"I think few means more than one, like maybe three or four," Candace said.

Derek, an observant first grader, noted, "I think 'a few' means about five seconds because when we were playing *Wiggly Wobbly,* I watched the red hand on the clock."

"Derek is right," I said. "I timed five seconds the first time we played the game, and I also timed five seconds after the game when you wiggled for one whole minute."

To clarify the idea of "a few," I said, "Quietly stand up if you rode the bus to school today." Most of the children stood up, as I knew they would, and I commented, "Almost *all* of you rode the bus," emphasizing "all." I then said, "OK, now stand up if you did not ride the bus to come to school today." Five students stood. I continued, this time emphasizing "few": "So, only a *few* children didn't ride the bus today. Here 'a few' means five. Now stand up if you are wearing a ribbon in your hair today." Three girls stood and I explained, "This time 'a few' means three. The exact number can change, but 'a few' means not very many of what we have."

I then returned to the activity: "Let's think of things you could do in about five seconds." I started a new list on the board: *after five seconds,* and recorded as the children shared. Their suggestions included "blow a bubble," "write my name," "count to ten," "sing about half of the ABC song," "line up," "draw a star or happy face," "eat some M&M's," and "read the title of the book *Before and After.*"

Next I wrote on the board: *after five minutes* and *after one hour.* The students gasped as they anticipated what it would feel like to wiggle and wobble for those lengths of time.

"How many minutes are in one hour?" I asked. Most of the children knew and I wrote on the board: *1 hour = 60 minutes.*

As the students offered ideas for tasks that could be done in the two new categories of elapsed time, I recorded on the lists. For *after five minutes,* they offered "eat breakfast," "ride my bike to school," "walk to school," "find a book to read," "brush my teeth and get ready for bed," "eat a piece of pizza," "run up and down the football field once," and "get my brother in trouble." For *after one hour,* they suggested "watch a movie," "play outside with my friends," "open birthday presents and eat cake," "go to lunch," "make cookies," and "clean my desk." This last one received some giggles as Logan, who suggested it, has an extremely disorganized desk.

After compiling the four lists, I explained to the students that they were now going to draw pictures that showed elapsed time the way the drawings in the book do. "You can use an idea from the lists on the board, or another idea," I told them.

To model an example, I folded a piece of drawing paper in half and sketched a cookie on one half. "This is my 'before' picture. Now I'm going to drawn an 'after' picture to show what could happen to this chocolate chip cookie after some time passes." On the other half of the paper, I drew the cookie again, but with a bite taken out of it. I asked, "About how much time do you think could have elapsed from my 'before' picture to my 'after' picture for the cookie to have had one bite taken out of it—five seconds, one minute, five minutes, or one hour?"

The children answered unanimously, "Five seconds."

As they watched, I labeled the two sides of my example *before* and *after five seconds*. Then, to make sure that the students understood, I flipped the paper over. I drew a chocolate chip cookie on one half and a few crumbs on the other.

"How much time has elapsed in this picture?" I asked.

"A minute," most answered. "Five minutes," some said. I labeled the left side of my drawing *before* and the right side *after one minute*, explaining, "I love cookies and it would take me only one minute to eat one."

I then said, "Raise a hand when you have an idea about what you are going to draw and how much time will elapse." Most of the children decided on an idea immediately, some making up their own while others chose from the lists we had brainstormed. As students told me their ideas, I gave them pieces of white drawing paper and dismissed them from the rug to begin work.

Kaylee, Brenna, and Anthony each illustrated an elapsed time of five seconds. (See Figures 1–1, 1–2, and 1–3.) Julia struggled with her

Figure 1–1: Kaylee showed birthday candles before and after making a wish.

Figure 1–2: Brenna's piece of pizza had a bite missing after five seconds.

Figure 1–3: Anthony's illustration depicts an exciting moment in a hockey game.

Figure 1–4: Julia illustrated the writing and erasing process.

illustration for an elapsed time of one minute—would a person erase first and then write, or write and then erase? (See Figure 1–4.) She decided to draw three squiggly lines to represent writing for "Before," explaining, "Well, first you would write something and then get a better idea and have to erase." William's drawings showed something that could happen in five minutes. (See Figure 1–5.)

Math and Nonfiction, Grades K–2

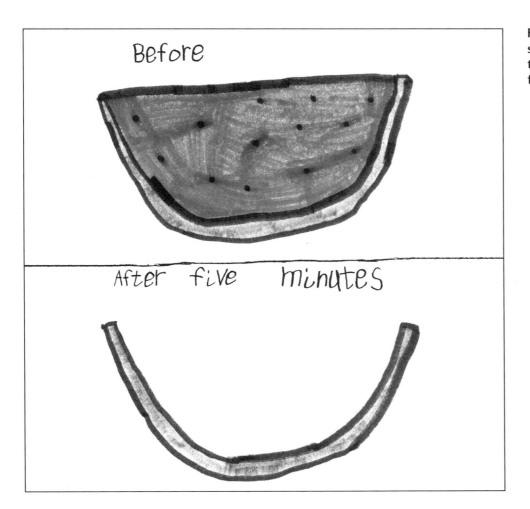

Before

After five minutes

The Second Lesson

This lesson involves students in observing what happens to an ice cube as time passes. I taught it to the same class of first and second graders about a month after the first lesson. I began just before lunch so that we could observe what happened to our ice cubes after one minute and five minutes, go to lunch, then return after lunch to check on what happened after one hour. I made the activity more manageable by dividing the class into two groups and starting one group on observing its ice cubes a few minutes before the other. This way I could monitor the students more easily.

As in the previous lesson, I began by sharing *Before and After*. The students enjoyed hearing the book again and participated as they had before by explaining what changed over time in each of the environments pictured.

"What do you suppose would happen to an ice cube if we took it out of the freezer?" I then asked.

"It would melt," the class agreed.

"About how much time would pass before it would start to melt?" I asked. The students' ideas ranged from one second to five minutes.

"About how much time do you think would elapse before the ice cube would be completely melted?" I asked. This time their ideas ranged from three minutes to one hundred minutes.

I explained that we were going to observe and record what happens to ice cubes after one minute, five minutes, and one hour. Taking a piece of white paper, I modeled for the children how to fold it into fourths and I labeled the four sections *before, after one minute, after five minutes,* and *after one hour.*

before	after one minute
after five minutes	after one hour

After they returned to their table groups, I gave each child a sheet of white paper and a clear plastic cup. I monitored as they folded their papers into fourths and labeled the four sections as I had. When all of the students had prepared their papers, I instructed them to think about what their ice cube would look like in the "before" sketch. I tipped the cooler so that the children could see the trays of ice cubes inside it. I said, "Draw in the first section on your paper what an ice cube looks like before we take it out of a tray in the cooler and before it starts to melt." I gave time for the children to do this.

Because telling time and keeping time were essential to the activity, I asked students to look at the wall clock. "Let's time one minute," I said. I waited until the red second hand was on the twelve and we counted aloud from one to sixty as it made one revolution. "That's one minute," I said. "There are sixty seconds in one minute."

"We will begin observing the ice cubes at 11:30. Then, *after one minute,* you will begin drawing what you notice happening," I said, pointing to the section on the paper that read *after one minute*. "You may notice very little change in your ice cube, but draw what you see and include any details you observe."

On the board, I wrote *11:30* and asked the students to copy this under the word *before* on their paper. I also wrote *11:31* and *11:35* and asked the children to record those times under *after one minute* and *after five minutes*. I then asked all the students to watch the wall clock and see when it got to 11:30 (less than a two-minute wait). When the time arrived, I removed a tray of ice cubes from the cooler, quickly dropped one cube into each student's cup, and prompted them to watch the time. "After one minute passes," I said, "draw how your ice cube looks."

The children grew silent as they watched both the second hand on the clock and their ice cubes. At 11:31, the entire class busily began recording pictures of their ice cubes after one minute. I encouraged the students to pick up their cups and peer through the bottom so that they could see any melting. As the students finished their sketches, they turned their attention to the wall clock, watching intently until the five-minute time period had elapsed.

After the students had drawn their pictures for "after five minutes," they went to lunch from 11:50 to 12:20. By leaving the experiment and coming back to it, the children gained a stronger sense of what can happen after one hour.

Upon returning to the classroom, the children rushed to their tables to check their cups. Nearly all of the ice cubes had melted. Most of the students were surprised to find that the ice cubes had melted completely. Some were surprised at how small an amount of water each ice cube melted into. The ice cubes that had not fully melted attracted much attention. All the students were eager to complete the experiment.

After the children settled in their seats, we checked the clock on the wall for the current time. It was about 12:25, which gave me a moment to recap what had happened before they went to lunch. Then I asked, "Our 'before' picture states that we began at 11:30, or half past 11:00. What time would one hour later be?"

Hands went up around the room. All the students were highly motivated by this activity and eager to answer, so I asked the class to answer in unison. I was prepared to hear some mixed responses.

"I heard you say, 'Now!' 'Half past 12:00' and '12:30.' You are all right, and it's almost that time." I wrote *12:30* under *after one hour* on the board, and asked the students to record the same time on their papers.

As soon as the clock's second hand ticked to 12:30, the students diligently began to draw the last of the four observations. A busy silence filled the room.

As the students completed their work, I gathered them on the rug and we revisited the book *Before and After*. We focused on the wetland setting because it shows one hour elapsing. We studied the changes and I read from the Nature Notes at the back of the book.

We talked about all that had happened in the last hour. I summarized on a piece of chart paper that we posted on our wall:

Things We Can Do in One Hour:

We folded paper, labeled it, drew our ice "before," recorded the times, got ice cubes, drew a picture for "after one minute," watched some more, drew a picture for "after five minutes," washed our hands, lined up, went to lunch, ate, played outside at recess, and returned to the classroom.

The students made good use of their melted ice cubes, watering the seeds we had planted in milk cartons a few days earlier. They stacked the cups to reuse another day.

In the weeks that followed, the students were very interested in how much time things took. When we started an activity, some would check the clock, either recording the time or making a mental note of it, and then would figure out how much time had elapsed when we finished. During the remainder of the school year, I occasionally asked students to record the time displayed on the wall clock and then write down what time it would be in thirty minutes. "That is the length of time you'll have to finish this activity," I would tell them.

I experienced another benefit from teaching this lesson: Whenever I would say something like, "It's time to clean up and I think it will take you about five minutes," my students had a better understanding of five minutes than they had before, and they would check the clock to try and get the job done in even less time.

Big and Little

Steve Jenkins's book *Big and Little* (1996) is about animals that are related to each other but quite different in size. The beautiful illustrations show animals at the same scale, making it easy to compare their sizes visually, and the book includes information about the animals being compared. At the back of the book, he presents a two-page spread of silhouettes of all the animals in the book along with a silhouette of a full-grown human, all drawn to scale. The book provides a springboard to providing kindergarten children an experience with measurement.

MATERIALS

I read *Big and Little* aloud to a class of kindergartners early in the school year. The students had been collecting data about each other and using the information to create pictographs that we posted on the wall. I referred to the graph about the children's pets, to begin this lesson.

"I notice from our graph that many of you have pets. Some of you have dogs, cats, and fish, and three of you have a gerbil or hamster at home," I said. "If you have a gerbil or a hamster, would you come up and stand next to me?" I chose these two animals, which are rodents and related to mice, because they are similar in size but also have differences.

If the students had not previously graphed pets, I would have had a conversation with them, asking how many of them had ever seen a rodent and inquiring about how you might hold one. My objective was to get students to begin thinking about the size, similarities, and differences of related animals. A conversation about dogs would also work well, as most students are very familiar with dogs and the vast variety of breeds.

Three students came up to stand next to me. Michael said that he had a pet hamster; Sarah and Tamara had gerbils. I asked them to show their classmates how they would hold their pet in their hands. Each cupped his or her hands together.

"What do you know about the size of their pets?" I asked the audience of kindergartners. Their hands went up eagerly.

"They're small," Lenny stated.

"They're little," replied Hima.

"Tiny," blurted Rodney.

I nodded to agree with each comment, then asked Michael, Sarah, and Tamara, "Are gerbils and hamsters alike? How are they the same and how are they different?"

"A hamster doesn't have a tail but a gerbil does," Michael said proudly.

"My gerbil has a tail like a mouse. My mom doesn't like it," revealed Sarah.

"Oh," I said, "so a gerbil is like a mouse because they both have tails. And gerbils and hamsters are different because a gerbil has a tail but a hamster doesn't."

"Yes," Michael and Sarah agreed.

I thanked the three students for helping me and asked them to join the others sitting. "Would all of you show how you would hold Michael's pet hamster?" All of the students cupped their hands carefully in front of them. "Now show me how you might hold Sarah's or Tamara's gerbil." A few students looked at their classmates to make sure they hadn't misunderstood as their hands remained the same. "Do you know that hamsters, gerbils, and mice have a relative that is so big it couldn't even fit in your lap, let alone your hands?"

"No," the children chorused. Surprised gasps and giggles filled the room.

I continued, "Some rodents, like hamsters, gerbils, and mice, are little, but some rodents are very big. You'll learn about one when I read this book to you." I asked the children to put their hands in their laps and then I showed them the book.

"*Big and Little* is the title of the book I'm going to share with you today. In this book you'll see and learn about animals that are related but very different in size. Some animals are really little," I squeaked in a high whisper, "and others are very, very big," I boomed in a low, loud voice. The children giggled and wiggled, eager to listen.

I skipped the author's note at the front of the book, which explains why animals of the same species vary in size and talks about the scale of the illustrations. I believe that this information is too advanced for kindergartners and not significant to the lesson. I showed the children the spread of the Siamese cat and the Siberian tiger, reading, "When hunting, the Siamese cat acts like its wild cousin, the Siberian tiger." I stopped to let the children enjoy the beautifully colored collage artwork, then read the text a second time.

Alexis said, "My brother said to me that tigers are attracted to cats."

"Tigers are attracted to cats?" I questioned.

"I mean related to cats," Alexis corrected herself.

As I turned the page, I asked the children to pay special attention to the sizes of the animals in the book. The next spread pictures a ruby-throated hummingbird and an ostrich, also showing that the Siamese cat is larger than a hummingbird and smaller than an ostrich. Again, I read the text twice and gave the children time to enjoy the artwork.

I repeated this procedure for the next spread, which shows the Nile crocodile and the African chameleon. Turning the page to show a capybara, the world's largest rodent, and a deer mouse, I read, "The capybara weighs as much as one thousand deer mice."

Jesse said, "He looks like a rat."

"Would a rat be bigger or smaller than the capybara?" I asked.

"Smaller," the class chorused.

"And my hamster at home would be smaller," Tamara assured us.

As I continued reading, the students commented on the different sizes of the animals. After talking about the last two animals, the sea otter and the elephant seal, I turned the page to reveal a two-page layout that shows silhouettes of all the animals in the book, plus the silhouette of a human adult, all drawn to the same scale.

"Here are all the animals that were in this book," I said to the class.

One observant kindergartner blurted, "There wasn't a man in the book."

I responded, "You're right. There wasn't a man in the book, but his picture helps you see what size your mom or dad would be standing next to these animals."

"I see some animals that are bigger than the man," Cole said.

"I see some that are small," said Julieta.

I then told the children what they were to do next. "I'm interested in what you know about *big* and *little*. Just as Steve Jenkins did in this book, I'd like you to draw two animals that are related somehow, but one should be really little and the other really big."

One boy raised his hand, "Do they have to be related?"

"Yes," I replied. "For example, they could both be cats. If you were going to draw cats, what might you draw for your big cat? Alisa?"

"A leopard."

"I would draw a tiger," Darin said, then roared like a tiger.

"What kind of cat could you draw for the little cat?" I asked.

"I would draw my cat. He's black with white right here," described Joe, rubbing his neck.

The children began to get excited about their drawings. After they were back in their seats and had their crayons out, I asked one student from each table to come up to the front of the room. With the others watching, I showed these children how to fold a sheet of white drawing paper in half by matching the corners and then creasing. Each child carefully folded a sheet as I had modeled. I then showed them how to label one side of the paper with a *B* for "big" and the other with an *L* for "little." The children then returned to their tables, the experts for their groups, and helped others fold their pieces of paper in half. In a few moments, the entire class had set to work on their drawings.

I walked around the classroom, checking in with students and talking with them about their drawings. Tamara had not yet labeled her work but was working hard coloring her two drawings. I noticed that the drawings were very similar in size and asked Tamara about them.

"It's a shark," she said pointing to the fish on the "big" half of the paper, "and a goldfish," pointing to the "little" side. "A shark is a big fish and a goldfish is a little fish."

When I came back to Tamara's table later, she was diligently labeling her drawings *HSRK*—shark—and *GOID*—gold, for goldfish. (See Figure 2–1.) This confirmed that Tamara understood big and little, although her drawings were nearly the same size.

Emma's drawing was nearly complete when I got to her. She had drawn two similar cats, with one clearly bigger than the other. Emma was eager for me to see her work and told me, "I drew two cats. A tiger and my cat." (See Figure 2–2.)

Figure 2–1: Tamara's work showed a big fish—a shark—and a little fish—a goldfish.

Figure 2–2: Emma drew a big tiger and a little house cat.

Most kindergarten students completed this activity with little guidance. The challenging part for some was choosing animals that were related. Emma and Tamara's drawings represent the work that this group of kindergartners completed. The products demonstrate the developmental stage where children are beginning to understand the ideas of size and measurement.

Biggest, Strongest, Fastest

Biggest, Strongest, Fastest, by Steve Jenkins (1995), introduces some of the biggest, strongest, and fastest animals that roam our earth. There is an illustration, simple text, and facts for each animal, plus small silhouettes that compare the animal to a full-grown human, an adult's open palm, or, in one instance, lightbulbs.

In the first of the two lessons described here, second graders use their own hand spans as a nonstandard unit of measure to compare with the lengths of various objects in the classroom. The second lesson is a measurement activity that is suitable for kindergartners.

MATERIALS

First Lesson

6-by-6-inch squares of black construction paper, 1 per student

8-by-8-inch square of black construction paper, 1 for demonstration

1 teaspoon

white crayons

Second Lesson

Animals worksheet, 1 per student (see Blackline Masters)

The First Lesson

Biggest, Strongest, Fastest is an ideal book for helping children develop an understanding of length. I gathered the second graders and read the book aloud, sticking strictly to the simple text and not reading the additional information about each animal or pointing out the small silhouette illustrations that depict each animal's special record.

After finishing the book, I prepared the children for the lesson I had planned by returning to certain pages and showing how Jenkins had used silhouettes of hands and animals to compare their sizes.

The first spread I revisited showed the Etruscan shrew. I read, "The Etruscan shrew, the world's smallest mammal, could sleep in a teaspoon. From the tip of its nose to the end of its tail, this shrew is only two and a half inches long. It weighs about as much as a Ping-Pong ball."

I directed the students' attention to the tiny silhouette of a shrew next to a silhouette of an open hand. I said, "Look how the length of the Etruscan shrew compares to the grown-up's hand." The students' eyes grew big, and many of them commented on the remarkably small size of the animal.

I held up the teaspoon I had brought for the lesson. "This mammal could sleep in a teaspoon," I reminded the children.

"Woo," the students uttered in amazement at the small size of the spoon.

Jonathan exclaimed, "My hamster could about fit in that spoon." I thanked Jonathan and moved on to show the class the next page in the book.

I read the text that tells that the bee hummingbird is the smallest bird in the world. Then I read the additional facts and pointed to the silhouettes of a hummingbird and an open hand. The children were amazed to learn that the bee hummingbird weighs less than a dime does.

Another page compares the bird spider and the flea to an open hand. When we looked at the silhouettes of the bird spider and the hand, the children noticed that they were about the same size. I held up my hand and spread my fingers apart. I said, "Wow, that is a huge spider! Most spiders I've seen are about the size of my pinky nail." The students looked carefully at my fingernail and nodded in agreement. Many of them inspected their own hand spans.

I explained what they were going to do next: "Now your task is to find things in the classroom that are about as long as the reach of your own hand span. Show me how wide you can open your hand." The students held up their hands, fingers spread apart.

I wanted to be sure that the students understood how to use their hand span to measure, so I explained and demonstrated. First I placed my spread-out left hand on the board and marked the tip of my pinky and the end of my thumb.

I removed my hand and drew a line between the two marks I had made. "This line shows the length of my hand span," I said. "Your hand span measures from your pinky to your thumb."

"Now let me see if I can find something that is about as long as my hand span," I continued. "I'll try the book we've been reading." I held up the book and measured the cover in both directions. The left edge, along the spine, was just about the same as my hand span; the bottom edge was longer than my hand span.

"Now see if you can find things in the room that are just about the same length as your hand span," I said.

I let the students explore freely around the classroom for about ten minutes. They became very involved. At first they seemed to be just walking around randomly measuring items with their hands. Soon their searches became more methodical, with the children moving directly toward items that they thought would be about as long as their hand spans.

When we came back together on the rug, all of the students had experienced some success at finding things that were about the same length as their hand spans. I explained how we were going to share all of our findings.

First I demonstrated how to trace a hand. I taped an 8-by-8-inch square of black construction paper on the board, then used a piece of chalk to trace the outline of my open left hand. I removed the square from the board and carefully cut out the pattern of my open hand. "Now I'll use my cutout hand to find something in the classroom that is just about the same length," I said.

I had already done a search in the room and found that my hand span was about as long as one of our computer speakers. But I began modeling for the class by purposely measuring something that I knew was shorter than my hand span—the light switch. I held my cutout hand up to it, saying, "I thought this light switch would be about the size of my hand."

"No!" the kids roared.

Toby followed with, "Your hand is too big."

"Your hand is bigger than the light button, but it's close," Conner said. Although Conner and a few other students thought that the light switch was "close enough," I told them that the task was to find something closer in measure: "I'm looking for something that's almost exactly the same length as my hand span."

Next I held my cutout hand next to the pencil sharpener that hangs on our wall, knowing that it was also close but not long enough. I wanted to emphasize again that I was looking for an object that was almost exactly as long as my hand span.

Finally, I went to a computer speaker and showed the class that my hand span was nearly the exact length of one side of the speaker. To mark my finding, I rolled a piece of masking tape and stuck my cutout hand to the side of the speaker.

I then reviewed with the students what they were to do. "First trace your hand span onto black paper using your white crayon. Then cut it out carefully, so it's as close as possible to your actual hand. Next use your cutout hand to measure items in the room. Once you find an item that is nearly the same length as your hand span, get a piece of masking tape, roll it, and carefully tape your cutout hand on or next to the object."

The students returned to their seats and got to work tracing their hands onto 6-by-6-inch black paper squares and then cutting out their hands. The majority of the children traced their hands with ease. These students were very helpful to their peers who needed assistance to trace their own hands accurately. All of the students were able to cut out their paper hands, with only a couple having to tape on a finger that got torn off.

Our class became a roomful of hand silhouettes. After all of the students had taped their cutout hands somewhere in the room, we did a "museum walk" around the room, looking at all the items with hands taped on them. For each, I asked whose hand it was so that the students were recognized for their discoveries.

Throughout the week I observed many students using their hands to measure other things around the room. Some started to measure objects that were much longer than one of their hand spans.

"Our student desks are fourteen hands high," I overheard Carolina reporting to Andy and Jamal.

"No, they're fourteen and a half hands high," Andy protested.

Jamal tried to resolve the dispute by measuring the height of a student desk himself. He announced, "I got twelve. Well, a little more than twelve, but not thirteen." Carolina and Andy looked puzzled because they had watched Jamal measure and saw that he was measuring correctly. It didn't occur to them that the differences in their hand sizes was the reason for the different measurements. Soon all three were measuring again, checking the accuracy of their initial measurements.

Later I talked with the class about the different lengths of their hand spans and the need to have standard measures, like rulers, if we want to know how long something really is.

The Second Lesson

As I had with the second graders, I read the simple text in *Biggest, Strongest, Fastest* aloud to the kindergartners and showed them the illustrations. I then reread the book, also reading some of the additional facts included on each page or just referring to the silhouettes to draw the children's attention to the enormity or fragility of the animal's size.

These kindergartners had visited the zoo earlier in the year, and I asked them to recall zoo animals that were larger than their hands and animals that were smaller than their hands. I held up a copy of the blackline master that I had prepared. I pointed to the short phrase on each side of the paper and read, "Smaller than my hand. Larger than my hand." Each student received a copy of the Blackline Master. I told the students to draw an animal below each label. As they worked, I encouraged them to write the names of the animals depicted.

Animals

smaller than my hand . . .   larger than my hand . . .

I also taught this lesson to a group of kindergartners who hadn't been to the zoo. Focusing on the animals in the book led us to a discussion of other wild animals the students were familiar with. Although the children didn't have the shared zoo-going experience as a basis for their knowledge about animals, they listened to one another and drew on each other's ideas.

Can You Count to a Googol?

Robert E. Wells's *Can You Count to a Googol?* (2000) is a counting book that focuses on powers of ten and just how big those numbers are. The book begins with the number 1, the first counting number, and continues with 10; 100; 1,000; and so on. Each new number is presented three ways—symbolically with a numerical explanation, through a contextual situation, and with an illustration. In this lesson for first and second graders, students measure a stack of ten pennies, use that measurement to figure out how tall a stack of one thousand pennies would be, and represent the height of the thousand-penny stack with a strip of adding machine tape.

MATERIALS

pennies, 100 for each group of 2–3 students

adding-machine tape

1–100 chart (see Blackline Masters)

classroom number line

interlocking cubes, 100

base-ten blocks, at minimum one cube, one
   ten-unit block, and one hundred–unit block

"Today we are going to read a book about numbers—big numbers," I said to a class of first and second graders to begin the lesson. "What are some big numbers you know?"

"A hundred," Sari said.

"One million," Bruce countered.

"Nine hundred ninety-nine is a big number that I know," Cameron said.

As each student offered a number, I wrote it on the board first with numerals and then with words. I did this to help the students begin to make the connection between written and symbolic mathematical language.

Next I said, "I know a really, really big number—a *googol*. A googol is a number that's so big, I may not have enough space on the board to write it on the board because it has so many digits." I held up *Can You Count to a Googol?* and continued, "I'm going to read this book to you. It can help you learn about really big numbers and also about how big a googol is." Some of the children's eyes grew large in anticipation.

I began reading the book aloud and the students listened intently. The first page presents the number one and begins, "If you're looking for a really big number, it certainly won't be 1." The next page introduces the number ten, and the following page introduces one hundred. Although the book does a nice job of explaining how these numbers grow, I thought that it would be valuable to give the children different ways of looking at one, ten, and one hundred. I asked the students to identify each of the numbers in four ways: on a large 1–100 chart, on our classroom number line that extends across the front of the room, with base-ten blocks, and with interlocking cubes.

For the number one, first I called on Thomas to color in the one on the 1–100 chart. Next Angelica hung a clothespin from the one on the classroom number line. Finally, Xaviar and Julia showed the number using base-ten blocks and interlocking cubes.

I repeated this for ten, and then for one hundred. The book's page for one hundred shows eagles in ten groups of ten each. I asked the students what they observed about how the eagles are grouped. Several hands went up.

"Whisper to your neighbor how you think the eagles are grouped," I said. Soon the class was buzzing with the answer, that the eagles are in groups of ten. First we counted the groups to establish that there were ten groups of ten eagles on the page. Then I pointed to each group as the students counted by tens verifying that there were indeed one hundred eagles in all.

The text on the next spread says, "10 × 100 is 1,000. If ONE HUNDRED penguins each had TEN scoops of ice cream in a cone, that would be ONE THOUSAND scoops of ice cream." The illustration shows one hundred penguins standing on icebergs, ten to an iceberg, with each penguin holding an ice cream cone with ten scoops.

"What do you notice about the illustration?" I asked.

Lucy reported correctly, "I notice ten penguins on each piece of ice, and every penguin has an ice cream cone, and they all have ten scoops."

"Oh," I said, "on the last page we saw that ten groups of ten eagles were one hundred, so ten penguins each with ten scoops must mean that there are one hundred scoops of ice cream on each iceberg. Let's make sure." We spent the next few minutes first counting by tens the scoops of ice cream on one iceberg, and then counting scoops by hundreds until we got to one thousand scoops.

Can You Count to a Googol? continues the pattern of powers of ten through one trillion, and then explains how adding zeroes can increase one trillion to a quadrillion, a quintillion, and an octillion. Finally the googol is introduced as a "terrifically huge, amazingly stupendous, gigantic, mammoth-sized number" that has one hundred zeros.

After reading about the googol, I skipped the next two pages, titled "How Do We Know?" and concluded by reading the author's note at the back. Wells explains that a googol is one with a hundred zeros. It was first written down in the late 1930s by an American mathematician, Dr. Edward Kasner. Dr. Kasner asked his nine-year-old nephew, Milton, to give the number a name, and Milton called it a googol. My students were very surprised to hear that a nine-year-old boy was responsible for naming this number with one hundred zeros.

To introduce the activity, I returned to the two pages I had intentionally skipped, which clarify the measurements and sizes of items in the book's earlier pages. For example, we had seen one million illustrated by a crate filled with one million dollar bills, with children pictured next to the crate to give a sense of its size. I now read,

How do we know how big a stack 1,000,000 dollar bills would make? 1,000 new, unwrinkled dollars make a stack about 4 inches high. 10,000 make a stack about 40 inches high.

I then told the class, "Today we are going to discover how tall a stack of one thousand pennies would be. But we don't have enough pennies for you to actually stack one thousand. Instead I will just give you a handful. What do you suppose you could find out with just a handful of pennies?" Because we had counted by tens and hundreds during the reading of the text and then read about how the dollar bills were stacked and then measured, the students had some good ideas about how to do this task.

Angelica shared her idea first: "We could stack ten pennies and then measure how tall ten is, and then add that ten times to see what a hundred pennies would be and then keep going."

"What do you mean 'keep going'?" I questioned. Angelica started over again, explaining further this time.

"Well, I would know how much just ten is, and then I would find out how much one hundred is, and then I would just keep going until I got to a thousand."

"Would you keep going by tens?" I probed.

Figure 4–1: Angelica and
Stephanie's thinking.

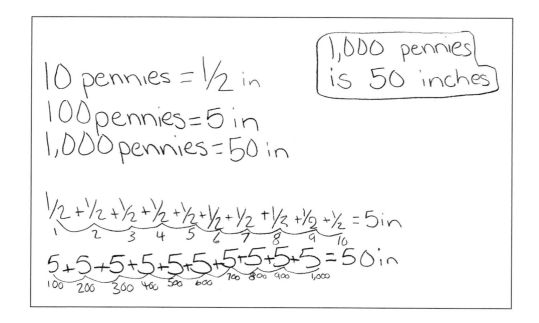

Figure 4–2: Thomas and
Brenna recorded the
problem differently.

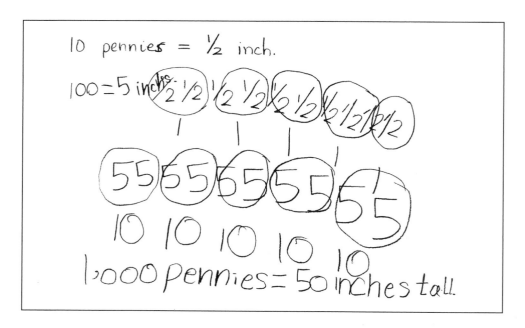

Angelica responded, "No, I would count by hundreds once I knew how much that was." (See Figures 4–1 and 4–2.)

Satisfied that Angelica had a clear idea of her plan, I called on Deshawn to explain his idea of how to solve this problem.

"I would find out how many pennies make one inch," he said.

"Why an inch?" I asked.

"Because I like to work with easy numbers when I measure, and one is an easy number for me," Deshawn clarified. Deshawn's work shows he discovered twenty pennies stacked upon the others equals one inch. (See Figure 4–3.)

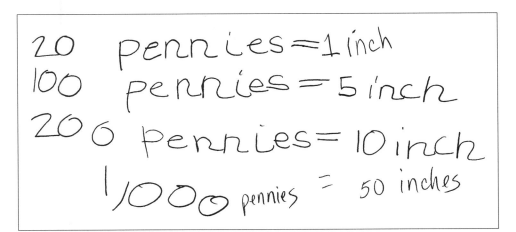

Figure 4–3: Deshawn used 1 inch because "one is an easy number."

After the students had represented their thinking on paper, they measured and cut strips of adding-machine tape so they could see how tall a stack of one thousand pennies would be. I asked the children how they might label their strips. As they made suggestions, I recorded their ideas on a piece of chart paper, first asking, "Should I write the number using digits or words?" Here are some of the sentences from our chart:

One thousand pennies is fifty inches tall.
1,000 pennies = 50 inches
Fifty inches is the height of a thousand pennies.

The students used many skills during this lesson. They measured, computed, and did some predicting and estimating. All of the children, no matter their facility with numbers, were able to participate in solving the problem.

City by Numbers

Taught by Bobbi Miest

In *City by Numbers* (1998), Stephen T. Johnson presents a collection of paintings that were inspired by outdoor urban landscapes in New York City. Each painting in this wordless picture book has one of the numerals from zero to twenty-one hidden in it—a three in the curves of a wrought-iron gate, a four in the span of the Manhattan Bridge, an eight formed by two wire trash bins, and so on. Young students enjoy searching for the numerals formed by buildings, benches, trees, even windowpanes. In this lesson, Bobbi Miest's kindergartners visually identify and trace with their fingers the numerals from one to twenty. The lesson is suitable for any young students who are working on numeral recognition.

MATERIALS

Earlier in the year, Bobbi had read *Alphabet City*, the companion book to *City by Numbers*, to her kindergarten class. When she showed *City by Numbers* to the children, many immediately made the connection.

"It's a number city," Oscar yelled.

The students gathered on the carpet, excited about looking for numerals in pictures of a city just as they had earlier looked for letters. Bobbi said, "As you did with *Alphabet City*, you need to use your 'I spy' eyes to look for numerals in this city. Let's practice with the cover. When you think you spy the number hidden on the cover raise your hand."

Every hand went up. The illustration on the cover shows two wire trash bins that touch, creating the numeral eight. Bobbi called on Thomas.

"I think it's one," said Thomas.

"A one might be on the first page," said Bobbi, "but what number do you spy on the cover?" Bobbi gestured to the cover. "Molly, what do you spy?"

"A zero," replied Molly.

"There are two zeroes," added Rachel.

"You're both right," Bobbi said, "but watch as I trace with my finger." With her index finger, Bobbi traced the rims of the two bins—the zeroes that Rachel saw—following the path we use to write the numeral eight.

"What number do you see?" Bobbi asked.

"Eight," the children chimed. Tracing the rims in one continuous motion like this helped all of the students see the numeral eight in the illustration.

Bobbi again traced the eight, singing a short rhyme about forming the numeral as she traced. Some of the students spontaneously drew the number in the air while others gently sang along: "We make an S but do not wait, go back up and close the gate."

Bobbi opened the book to a two-page spread of the Manhattan Bridge and asked, "What number do you spy this time?"

"It's a four," Ben offered.

"Who else sees a four?" Bobbi asked. About half of the children raised their hands.

"And who would like to come up and trace the four in this painting the way I traced the eight on the cover?" Bobbi asked.

Sasha came up and traced the four. As she did so, Ben added, "It's a very *long* four," emphasizing the word long.

Bobbi said, "There aren't any words at all in this book, so we're going to read it with our 'I spy' eyes. Your job is to find the number on each page. When you think you spy the number, raise your hand."

Bobbi showed the children a painting of a tall, thin building in the middle of other buildings. "When you spy the number, raise your hand," she said, repeating the direction. After a few moments, most of the children had a hand raised.

"Let's say the number together in a whisper voice," Bobbi said.

"One," most of the children whispered.

"Who would like to come up and trace the one?" Bobbi asked. David came up and ran his finger from the top to the bottom of the building.

"Let's all trace a one in the air," Bobbi said, and the children all did so.

Bobbi turned the page to show two paintings, side by side. The right-hand page clearly showed the numeral three in a wrought-iron gate, but the numeral on the left-hand page wasn't as obvious. The children weren't certain what the left-hand painting showed. Some thought leaves, others thought torn paper, one thought spilled paint.

"Who spies the number?" Bobbi asked. "Travis?"

"I spy a two," he said proudly.

Bobbi continued, "Who would like to come up and trace the two?" Sharon came up and traced it.

"Let's all trace a two in the air," Bobbi encouraged, and the children did so.

"And what about this painting?" Bobbi asked, pointing to the wrought-iron gate on the right-hand page. "Who spies a number?" Most of the hands shot up and Bobbi again had the class say the number together. When Purna came up to trace the three, she put her finger at the bottom of the numeral.

"Where do you start when you write a three?" Bobbi asked gently.

"Oh, yeah," Purna said, and moved her finger to the top of the gate. As with the other numbers, Bobbi then asked all of the children to trace a three in the air.

"So first we spied a one, then a two, and now a three," Bobbi said. "What number do you think will be on the next picture?" It was obvious to some children that four would come next, but others made random guesses. Bobbi turned the page and there was a gasp in the room when the children saw the bridge again.

"That's the four," Dillon said. Larissa came up and traced the four on the bridge, and then all the children traced a four in the air.

Bobbi asked, "Are there any guesses what city this four might be in?"

"A big city," said Akyme.

"Minneapolis," Jenna said, "and there's the Mississippi River." She pointed to the river in the picture.

"New York," said Grady.

"Or New Zealand," Alyssa offered.

Bobbi said, "This bridge is called the Manhattan Bridge, and it's in New York City. That's where Stephen Johnson, who painted all of these pictures, lives. And the river is called the East River."

Before turning the page, Bobbi told the students, "The next picture is tricky. What number do you think we are supposed to find?"

"Five," many replied. More of the children had figured out the counting pattern.

Bobbi turned the page to an illustration of a brick building on which shadows of tree branches create a five. The students quickly recognized the five. Ghada came up and traced the five, and all of the children traced it in the air.

Shadows created the numeral in the next picture, too. Rachel commented, "The shadows make the number six just like the number five. The shadow makes the long part of the six."

Bobbi continued through the book in the same way, having one child identify each number, having another trace it on the page, and then having all of the children trace it in the air.

The Coin Counting Book

The Coin Counting Book, by Rozanne Lanczak Williams (2001), is a fun introduction to coins, their value, counting, and computing. Photographs of actual coins complement the uncomplicated text. The book begins by introducing the penny, then shows that five pennies are equal to a nickel and ten pennies are equal to a dime. The author then explores combinations of coins that equal a quarter, a half dollar, and a dollar.

In the lesson described here, second graders discover different coin combinations that are equivalent to one quarter, which is exactly enough to purchase a carton of milk at lunch.

MATERIALS

coins, either real or play: approximately 500 pennies, 100 nickels, 50 dimes, and 25 quarters, divided so that each table has a supply

overhead coins

overhead transparency of a 1–100 chart

1–100 charts, 1 per student (see Blackline Masters)

optional: empty 8-ounce milk cartons, well rinsed, 1 per student

Before beginning to read *The Coin Counting Book*, I had prepared an overhead transparency of a 1–100 chart and had collected overhead coins. I planned to read just the first half of the book, through the section that deals with what coins are equivalent to a quarter.

I opened the book and showed the front and back covers to the second graders seated on the rug in front of me. The background of the front and back covers is a photographic image of a one dollar bill. Images of various coins are placed randomly on the bill. The cover captivated the children and their interest was evident. They marveled at the enlarged coins and the oversized dollar bill, and at their likeness to the "real thing."

To tie this lesson on money to something in the students' everyday lives, I planned to relate the amount of money we would talk about, twenty-five cents, to the price of milk cartons in the school cafeteria. If the milk in your cafeteria costs more or less than twenty-five cents, you could make the lesson relevant to your students' everyday lives by bringing in a lollypop or some other item that costs twenty-five cents. Or you could use your cafeteria's current milk price. The structure of the book would allow for this change, and your lesson need not hinge on building combinations of a quarter.

I began by saying, "You know the little milk cartons we buy in the cafeteria with our lunch each day?" I held up an empty 8-ounce milk container I had saved from the previous day and rinsed well. "How many of you know how much a container of milk costs?"

Nearly every student knew the answer, so I asked them to respond in unison. "A quarter!" replied most, with a few saying, "Twenty-five cents."

I said, "I heard some of you say 'a quarter' and others say 'twenty-five cents.'" I recorded on the board:

a quarter   25¢

"Which is it, a quarter or twenty-five cents? How much is this milk carton? Raise your hands please." I wanted to gauge how many students knew that these were both correct ways of naming the cost of a carton of milk. Most of the students put their hands up, some waving their arms to get noticed while others appeared less confident in their thinking.

"I think they're both right," Brecken began, "because twenty-five cents is the same as a quarter."

"A quarter is worth twenty-five cents, so you can say either. You can say the milk is a quarter or you can say it's twenty-five cents. Usually, though, Mrs. Johnson asks if we brought a quarter," Lauren informed us. Mrs. Johnson is the cashier in our cafeteria, so all of the students knew who Lauren was referring to.

"So a quarter is equivalent to twenty-five cents," I concluded as I inserted an equal sign to the information posted on the board.

a quarter = 25¢

I told the students that I was going to share just the first part of the book with them today, so they knew ahead of time that I would stop near the middle of the book. I hoped that preparing them this way would lessen any moans and groans there might be when I stopped reading before finishing the entire book.

As I read the simple, straightforward text of *The Coin Counting Book,* the students spontaneously began to read along with me on the pages that presented the equations; for example:

one penny + one penny + one penny + one penny
+ one penny = one nickel

If they hadn't done this, I would have encouraged them to do so. I directed students to read these equations twice since they're presented two ways in the text; the second representation for the example above was:

$$1¢ + 1¢ + 1¢ + 1¢ + 1¢ = 5¢$$

By the time I had reached the middle of the book, where I had intended to stop, the children were very involved in the reading.

"We can trade for one quarter, shiny and new," I read. "Two dimes and a nickel make one quarter, too. So do five nickels, five nickels for you!"

The students chimed in: "One dime plus one dime plus one nickel equals one quarter," they chorused. "Ten cents plus ten cents plus five cents equals twenty-five cents."

The students read the remainder of this page, which illustrates five nickels equaling a quarter. I then asked them to go back quietly to their tables. As they did so, I wheeled the overhead projector into place and pulled down the screen. With a transparency of a 1–100 chart projected, I asked, "How much is a penny worth?"

"One cent," the class replied, and I placed a transparent penny over the numeral one on the 1–100 chart.

"And two pennies?" I asked.

"Two cents," they answered, and I placed a second penny on the numeral two. We continued with two more pennies, covering the numerals three and four, too. Then I turned back to the second page of the book, reading, "One penny, two pennies, three pennies, four. What will we get when we add just one more?"

"Five pennies," Joseph replied.

"A nickel," added Jamison.

When I placed the fifth penny on the numeral five square of the chart, I also place a nickel on top of it. Because the coins were transparent, the students could see both representations—the five pennies and the nickel—at once.

1	2	3	4	5	6	7	8	9	10
11	12	13	14	15	16	17	18	19	20
21	22	23	24	25	26	27	28	29	30

I proceeded to put pennies over the numerals six, seven, eight, and nine. When we reached ten pennies, a few students' hands began to pop up as they anticipated the pattern we were creating. I placed a penny on the numeral ten and then asked, "What other coin could I place here?" To emphasize the answer I was looking for, I said, "I added one, two, three, four, five more pennies" as I pointed to the transparent pennies on top of the numerals six, seven, eight, nine, and ten on the 1–100 chart.

More students were now eager to share their ideas. Lilia began, "We should put a nickel there."

"Who can explain why we should put a nickel on the number ten?"

"Because five pennies equals a nickel, and we put down five more pennies," Darien replied.

Kelli agreed with this explanation and made the connection to skip counting, "We should put another nickel on ten because when we count by fives it goes five, ten, fifteen, twenty, like that. So I think we should put a nickel on ten."

Jamal recognized a pattern forming. "Ten should have a nickel because if you start with one, it goes penny, penny, penny, penny, penny *and* nickel, and then it repeats."

I placed a nickel on top of the penny on the ten square indicating the second group of five pennies covering the numerals six through ten, totaling five cents.

"What other coin could represent ten pennies or two nickels?" I asked.

Hands were waving wildly, so I called for the children to respond together. They triumphantly chorused, "A dime!" I placed a dime on the ten square of the 1–100 chart, indicating that ten pennies or two nickels is equal to one dime.

1	2	3	4	5	6	7	8	9	10
11	12	13	14	15	16	17	18	19	20
21	22	23	24	25	26	27	28	29	30

I removed the 1–100 chart from the overhead projector screen but left the ten pennies, two nickels, and one dime. I grouped five pennies together and asked, "What coin does this equal?"

"A nickel," Darien responded. I recorded:

one penny + one penny + one penny + one penny
+ one penny = one nickel

Next I grouped ten pennies into two groups of five and asked the children what this grouping showed.

Micah volunteered. I recorded his words as he spoke:

five pennies + five pennies = one dime

Then I grouped the two nickels together and asked, "What could I write to show what two nickels combined would be?"

Kelsey helped this time. I recorded what she said:

one nickel + one nickel = one dime

I then wrote each of the three sentences numerically under the original sentence, to prepare the students for what they would later do on their own. The overhead read:

one penny + one penny + one penny + one penny
+ one penny = one nickel
1¢ + 1¢ + 1¢ + 1¢ + 1¢ = 5¢

five pennies + five pennies = one dime
1¢ + 1¢ + 1¢ + 1¢ + 1¢ + 1¢ + 1¢ + 1¢ + 1¢ + 1¢ = 10¢

one nickel + one nickel = one dime
5¢ + 5¢ = 10¢

I then present the students with a problem to solve: "Now what I'd like you to do is discover different combinations of coins that equal one quarter. I want to see many different ways to buy a container of milk at lunch. You said that Mrs. Johnson usually asks for a quarter. Well, if you didn't have a quarter in your pocket but you had some pennies, nickels, and dimes, you might be able to purchase milk anyway because those coins could add up to twenty-five cents."

I explained that I wanted them to conduct this exploration by grouping coins or using 1–100 charts. I asked the students to take out their 1–100 charts in case they decided to use them. I placed a jar of coins on each table. Each jar contained mostly pennies but also had nickels, dimes, and just a few quarters. I said, "Experiment with the coins to find different combinations that add up to one quarter. Each group of coins should be worth twenty-five cents."

I gave the students time to investigate the coin combinations. While they did so I walked around the room making informal observations.

About three-fourths of these second graders seemed comfortable with mixing different combinations of coins to get twenty-five cents. The rest, however, used all pennies. I encouraged a few of those students to begin making trades by prompting them with questions like, "What if you took these five pennies and traded them in for one coin? What would that coin be?" Or, "I noticed you grouped your pennies into five groups of five. What coin is worth five pennies? Could you replace one of your groups with a nickel?"

Mohamed, for example, had counted out twenty-five pennies and grouped them into groups of five.

"I noticed you grouped your pennies into groups of five. How many pennies do you have here altogether?" I asked, wondering if he would count each coin (counting by ones) or count the groups of pennies (skip-counting by fives).

"The whole thing is twenty-five," he said.

"Show me how you know," I prodded.

Mohamed counted, placing his hand on top of each group of coins: "Five, ten, fifteen, twenty, twenty-five."

"That's a lot of coins," I said. "Are there any other coins in the money jar that you could trade one of these groups of five for?"

Mohamed thought about this as he looked into the jar of coins on the table. Finally he replied, "Yes."

"What coin is the same as five pennies? Show me your idea." I said.

"I can trade these five for a dime," Mohamed said, reaching for a nickel from the jar of coins.

"You're right," I confirmed. "You can trade five pennies for this coin, but it's not called a dime. Do you know what it's called?" Mohamed was comfortable taking risks. Had he not been, I would have simply told him that the coin he had selected was called a nickel, not a dime.

"Ummm . . . a nickel?" he answered uncertainly.

"Yes, it's a nickel," I replied.

After the students had investigated for about ten minutes, I gathered them on the rug again for further directions. Some of the children had created many combinations of coins totaling twenty-five cents. Others, like Mohamed, had struggled to create just one combination that equaled a quarter. I explained that today's activity would be to record just one of the ways they had discovered to make twenty-five cents. "I want you to record your combination of coins in three ways, just like in *The Coin Counting Book*."

I turned to the pages in *The Coin Counting Book* that depict using only pennies to equal a quarter. I chose this as an example because I had observed that a few students were comfortable thinking about it only in this way.

"See how this page illustrates three ways of showing a quarter? There are pictures of coins, words sentences, and number sentences. On these pages we can see that five groups of five coins make twenty-five. We then can read the words 'five pennies plus five pennies plus five pennies plus five pennies plus five pennies equals twenty-five pennies.' And we can read the number sentence, 'five cents plus five cents plus five cents plus five cents plus five cents equals twenty-five cents.' So you need to record in three ways—pictures of coins, a sentence using words, and a sentence using number and cent symbols."

We discussed how the children might draw their coins. I pointed out that in the book some coins showed the heads side of the coin and others the tails side. I emphasized that it was not necessary to add these details to their coins and they should not spend their time doing so. I said that they could trace around the real coins to make circles on their paper. We brainstormed ways they could show what coin each circle represented.

"We could put a *P* if it's a penny and an *N* for nickel and *D* for dime," Ethan suggested.

Ellie had a different idea: "Or you could just write how much it is worth on the coin, like for the nickel you could just write a five and a cent sign."

Tandee, who enjoys art, suggested, "We could color the coins. You could use your brown for the pennies and a gray crayon for the nickel and dime."

"How would you know which is the dime and which is the nickel if they are both gray?" I asked.

Other students raised their hands but I let Tandee clarify. "The dime is smaller than the nickel," she said matter-of-factly.

I asked if any of the children had questions before they went back to their seats. No one did, and they all seemed anxious to get back to their tables and get to work. I dismissed the students one by one by handing each a piece of 9-by-12-inch white paper, purposefully keeping for last students who had difficulty following multiple-step directions. This gave me a chance to check for understanding with each of them individually and give them extra help as needed. (Figure 6–1 shows Mohamed's work after my discussion with him. It shows four groups of five pennies and a nickel.)

I turned the overhead back on to give the children a visual reminder of the task. I also recorded the four coin words—*penny, nickel, dime,* and *quarter*—on cards and added those to the Word Wall where we collect words we use during classroom conversations. No major problems arose while the children were completing the task.

Camilla's work shows five nickels. (See Figure 6–2.) Camilla had one too many nickels in two of her sentences. I prompted her to double-check her work. She counted by fives and discovered that she had six nickels or thirty cents and erased one nickel.

Jimmy worked very independently and completed the task with ease using two dimes and a nickel. His representation of the coins depicts that he also knows a nickel is the larger of the two coins in size not value. (See Figure 6–3.)

We saved our milk cartons from lunch that day and used them to display our work. A couple of students rinsed each milk carton with

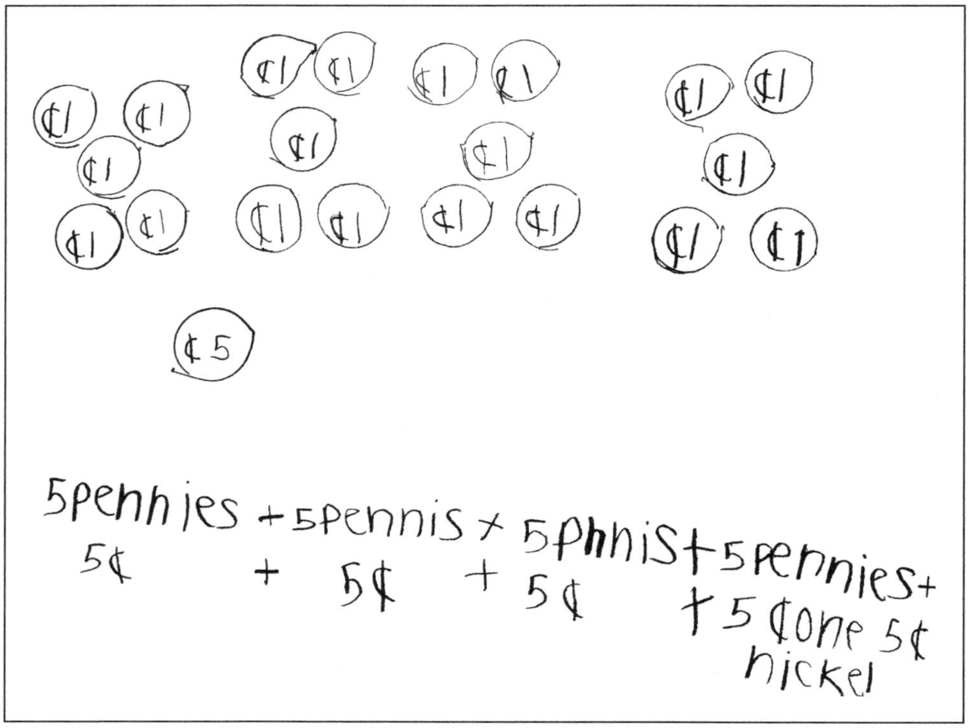

Figure 6–1: Mohamed learned that he could trade five pennies for a nickel. His illustration shows four groups of five pennies and one nickel equaling twenty-five cents.

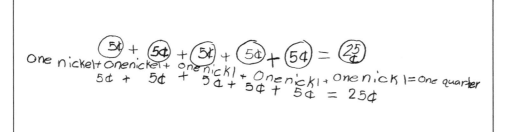

Figure 6–2: Camilla was comfortable counting by fives. She used nickels to total twenty-five cents.

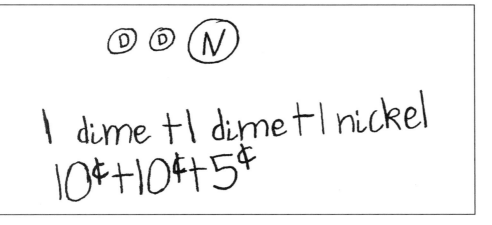

Figure 6–3: Jimmy was one of many students who were comfortable using mixed denominations of coins to equal twenty-five cents.

soap and water and let them dry overnight. A parent volunteer used a paper punch to put a hole through the top of each milk carton and the bottom of each student paper. The students then threaded the milk cartons to their papers using a small paperclip. We hung the work from our ceiling and enjoyed it for months.

You could also display the children's papers on a bulletin board in the classroom—or, better yet, hang them in the cafeteria next to the milk refrigerator to tie the mathematics to the students' real world. You could also combine the student papers into a classroom book, binding it and giving it a name like *How Much Is Milk? A Coin Counting Book*.

Color Zoo

Color Zoo, by Lois Ehlert (1989), is a Caldecott Honor book that uses bold colors and layers of cutout shapes to show the faces of different animals. Beginning with a cutout star, nine other cutout shapes reveal the animals, positioned so that as each page is turned, another picture is revealed. For example, a cutout circle is a tiger's face; turning the page leaves a cutout square that shows a mouse's face; turning the page again leaves a cutout triangle that is a fox's face. Three more series reveal other animals and shapes.

In this exploration, kindergartners listen to the book, then learn a card game that helps them become more familiar with the attributes and names of shapes.

MATERIALS

decks of 20 shape cards (2 of each of 10 shapes), 1 deck per pair of students (see *Color Zoo* Shapes in Blackline Masters)

shape cutouts made from 9-by-12-inch black construction paper, 1 each of the following shapes: star, circle, square, triangle, rectangle, heart, oval, diamond, octagon, hexagon

10 sheets of different colored 12-by-18-inch construction paper

1-quart zip-top bags, 1 per deck of cards

Lois Ehlert's book *Color Zoo* is ideal for introducing kindergartners to the names and attributes of two-dimensional shapes. Before reading this book to the class, I cut out each of the ten shapes introduced in the book from a sheet of 9-by-12-inch black construction paper and pasted each shape onto a sheet of brightly colored

12-by-18-inch construction paper. I planned to use these after reading the book as a reminder of and reference to the shapes introduced. I also prepared enough decks of shape cards so that I had a deck for every pair of students.

I used the hardback edition of *Color Zoo,* which begins with a star on the title page and has a total of ten shapes. The board book version doesn't include the star. If you use the board book with your class, you may want to eliminate the star from your decks of cards and construction paper cutouts.

I showed the children the cover of the book and asked, "What do you think this picture is?"

"A cat," Michael said.

"Maybe a bear," Lucy said.

"I think a cat," Emma said. "It has whiskers." She pointed to the orange whiskers.

I pointed out the shapes on the face. "Here's a circle," I said, tracing with my index finger. "And here's a square inside," I continued, tracing the square, "and here's a triangle in the middle." I traced it, too.

"The eyes are circles, too," David said.

"So are the ears," Nina said.

I opened the book to reveal the title page. The words *Color Zoo* peek through a cutout of a star. I turned the page with the star cutout and drew students' attention to the typed word *STAR* on the back of the page. "Color Zoo," I read, "by Lois Ehlert."

I read the first page and then turned it to show the children that the first illustration was the same picture as the one on the cover, but shown on three layers of pages, with a circle cut out of the top layer, a square cut out of the next, and a triangle cut out of the third layer. "The author of this book tells us here that this is a tiger's face," I said, pointing to the word *TIGER* in the bottom-right corner. I turned the page. The cutout circle then appeared on a black background on the left-hand page with *CIRCLE* written in the corner, and the picture on the right-hand page changed from the face of a tiger to the face of a mouse. I pointed to the word *MOUSE* in the lower right corner. I turned the page to show that the left-hand page had the cutout square on the black background with the word *SQUARE,* while the right-hand page showed the face of a fox with *FOX* written in the corner. Turning the page again revealed a cutout triangle on the left with the word *TRIANGLE* and just the two round eyes left on the right-hand page with the three shapes introduced underneath—square, triangle, and circle.

The next set of pages shows the faces of an ox, a monkey, and a deer, and introduces three new shapes—rectangle, oval, and heart. The final set of pages shows faces of a lion, a goat, and a snake, and introduces three more shapes—hexagon, octagon, and diamond.

After reading the book to the students, I posted on the board the ten 12-by-18-inch sheets of construction paper I had prepared, each with the silhouette of one of the shapes in the book. I arranged the shapes in the order they appeared in the book.

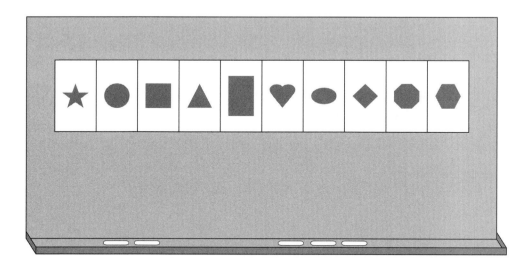

The students were familiar with the first seven shapes in the book—star, circle, square, triangle, rectangle, oval, and heart—and were able to name them easily. As they named a shape, I wrote its name on the brightly colored paper underneath its silhouette. To help the children with the names for the rest of the shapes, I reread the book so that students could again see each shape, hear its name, and see its name in print.

After I had labeled all ten posters, I told the students, "Now we're going to play a card game called *Shape Go Fish*. It's sort of like the game *Go Fish*. How many of you have ever played *Go Fish*?" Samantha was one of the students who raised a hand, so I selected her to come to the front of the room and demonstrate the game with me.

I explained, "To play, you'll have a deck of cards that are just like these large shapes posted on the board. The deck has two of each shape."

With the students gathered around in a circle, I mixed the twenty cards in one deck and dealt out four cards to Samantha and four to myself. I placed the remaining cards in a stack between us, face down.

"Now we each look at our cards," I explained. "The goal is to make pairs of shapes that are alike. If you are holding any two cards that are alike, place them face up in between us." Neither Samantha nor I had any pairs.

I then said to Samantha, "You can go first. Ask me for a shape that will give you a pair."

"Do you have a circle?" she asked.

"No," I replied, "go fish." Samantha knew to take one card from the stack between us.

"Now it's my turn to ask," I said. "Do you have a rectangle?"

Samantha did and gave the card to me. I laid my pair of rectangles face up, showing all the students how the shapes on the two cards matched. I explained, "When you make a match, it's still your turn, so I get to ask again."

Samantha and I continued playing until we had matched all ten shapes. Then I organized the students into pairs and distributed one deck of cards to each pair. I circulated and observed as they played.

Dillon and Mia had made three matches and Mia was out of cards, but Dillon still had cards and additional cards remained in the pile.

"I'm out of cards so Dillon can't ask me for anything. What should we do?" Mia inquired.

"Well, the goal is to make all the matches you can from the whole deck, so you should take a new card from the stack in the middle so you can still play and make matches," I replied.

This same situation occurred with another pair of students, so after we had finished playing *Shape Go Fish* and were putting the decks of cards into zip-top bags, I explained to all of the students what had happened with Dillon and Mia and how the game proceeds if that situation arises.

I asked the students what they had learned from playing *Shape Go Fish* with the shape cards. Their responses told me that they had learned about shapes, learned how to play the game, and developed strategies.

"I learned what an oval is, and it is kind of like a circle only longer," said Claire.

"I learned how to get a match," Tamika said. "See, if you keep asking for the same shape every time, then you will get it. That's what I do and it works."

A few of the kindergartners had had difficulty differentiating between the hexagon and the octagon. Each of the shape cards had the name of the shape printed on it, so I told them to look at the beginning letters of the words. This was the middle of the year and the children were familiar with the letters of the alphabet. If you were teaching this lesson at the beginning of the year, or if looking at the words didn't help a particular pair of students who were having difficulty with the hexagon and octagon cards, you might need to remove those cards from the deck.

I continued to use the decks of shape cards for the rest of the year. We didn't always play *Shape Go Fish*. Sometimes students would play *Concentration*, placing all of the cards facedown and then flipping pairs, trying to find a match. The students were challenged by this game as they flipped one card and then tried to recall where they had previously seen the same shape.

I also attached magnetic tape to the backs of shape cards from several decks so that I could easily attach them to the board and create patterns with them. I introduced this as part of our morning routine. Every morning I used the cards to begin a pattern of shapes on the board. As students entered the room I gave each a magnetic shape card. Once everyone had arrived, the students helped to continue the pattern. Whoever was holding the card that came next came up and positioned it on the board.

Each time I introduced a new way of using the shape cards, I reread *Color Zoo* to the class. With each reading, the students made new discoveries and connections about the shapes.

Cubes, Cones, Cylinders, and Spheres

In *Cubes, Cones, Cylinders, and Spheres* (2000), Tana Hoban introduces children to geometric shapes through photographs of things in the world, including houses, farms, cities, and more. The four shapes named in the title are depicted in the photographs with baseballs, sugar cubes, drums, boxes, hats, and other common objects.

The book is a wonderful springboard for two lessons that help second graders develop the vocabulary to name and describe these three-dimensional shapes, become familiar with their attributes, and relate three-dimensional objects to two-dimensional pictures. In the first lesson, students find pictures in magazines and create their own version of *Cubes, Cones, Cylinders, and Spheres*. In the second lesson, the students collect common objects that are examples of the shapes and write riddles about them.

MATERIALS

First Lesson

4 geometric solids, 1 each of a cube, cone, cylinder, and sphere

chart paper, 4 sheets

8-by-18-inch green construction paper, 1 sheet per student

8-by-17-inch white construction paper, 1 sheet per student

magazines with color illustrations and photographs, several per student (ask parents to donate old magazines that are colorful and suitable for young children to use for projects)

Second Lesson

4 geometric solids, 1 each of a cube, cone, cylinder, and sphere

paper grocery bags, 1 per student plus two extra (paper lunch bags could be used)

The First Lesson

Prior to the lesson, I collected four wooden solids—a cube, a cone, a cylinder, and a sphere. I wrote the name of each on a label and affixed it to the shape. I put the shapes in a box and placed the box near the rug so that I would have the solids at hand after we had gone through the book. I also posted four pieces of chart paper on the board, one for each shape, for recording the children's descriptions.

Day 1

I gathered the children on the rug and showed them the cover of *Cubes, Cones, Cylinders, and Spheres.* I didn't read the title of the book but began by saying, "This book is filled with beautiful photographs of objects that I think you'll recognize. But the book doesn't have any words, so I need your help telling the story. With your whisper voices, we'll read the book together by naming the objects in each picture. Let's practice on the first page together."

I opened to the first page, a close-up of children's blocks, some with letters and numbers and some in different colors without anything written on them. "Blocks," most students whispered. "Cubes," a few said.

I turned the page and pointed to the photograph on the left-hand side. "Ice cream cones," they whispered.

When I pointed to the photo on the right-hand side, the children were quiet. "Does anyone have an idea?" I asked. George's hand shot up. "Smokestacks?" he asked, tentatively. I nodded, and he was pleased.

We continued this way and the students identified cones, bubbles, lights, a hot-air balloon, drums, dice, a globe, hats, sugar cubes, gift boxes, and baseballs. The children enjoyed their role in "reading" the story. A few photos, such as the one that shows a silo next to a barn, were troublesome for the children because they weren't familiar with the objects. To help with these, I explained where the picture might have been taken or in this case what a silo was used for. They were able to tell it was cylindrical in shape but I told them it was called a silo.

After we had looked at the entire book, I asked, "Now that you have looked inside the pages of this book, what do you think a good title for this book might be?"

"*The City and the Country,*" Rebecca offered.

"*Things You See,*" Frankie said thoughtfully.

"*Different Shapes.* Because there are a lot of different shapes in the book that make different things," Annabel reasoned.

I then pulled the wooden cube from the box. I said, "Cubes were shown in many of the photographs in this book. I'm going to let you inspect this cube using two of your senses—sight and touch. With your eyes and hands tell me how you would describe this shape." As students began to pass the cube, I wrote *Cube* at the top of one of the pieces of chart paper.

"It has six sides," Margaret began.

"Do you mean these?" I asked, pointing to the cube's square faces. Margaret nodded. "They're called the cube's *faces*," I said.

"Yeah, and the sides, I mean the faces, are all squares," Olivia added.

"It's shaped like a box," Mark said.

I recorded their ideas on the chart, paraphrasing to use the correct terminology.

six faces
faces are all square
shaped like a box

I continued until all of the students had had a chance to touch the cube and, if they wanted, contribute to our chart. I repeated the exercise for the other three shapes, introducing their names and creating a chart for each.

Then I suggested to the class that we read the book again. "This time," I said, "let's read the book by using the name of the shape of the object." I read the titles of the four charts as I pointed to them: "'Cube, cone, cylinder, sphere.' We need to use our whisper voices again. Let's practice on the cover."

The cover is a good place to start because all four of the shapes appear on it. As I pointed to the different objects in the photograph, the students whispered each shape's name in unison. I pointed to the boxes first. "Cube," whispered most of the students. Then I pointed to the orange construction cone in the background. "Cone," nearly everyone whispered. Then I motioned to the trash cans and the sticks of sidewalk chalk the kids in the photo are playing with. "Cylinders," the children chorused. The students said, "Sphere" when I pointed to the basketball and other balls on the cover. We then read the rest of the book in this way.

Next I said, "Today you'll each begin making your own *Cubes, Cones, Cylinders, and Spheres* book." The children's excitement was evident. "For your photographs, you'll search for these four shapes in magazines and cut them out. Then you'll use what you cut out for the pages of your book. Today we'll just look for and cut out our pictures. Tomorrow we'll organize our pictures into books."

I showed the children a piece of green construction paper that I had cut to 8 inches by 18 inches. "Watch as I fold this sheet," I said. "You'll do the same with your sheet of paper, and this will be the cover of your book." I folded the sheet in half and held it up to show that it was about the same size and shape as the back cover of the book. I said, "I chose the size and color deliberately to match Tana Hoban's book."

I then chose a few children to demonstrate how they would fold the green paper. I chose students who would need assistance in matching up the corners of the paper and creasing; this way I could help then while providing models for the rest of the class.

I directed the students' attention to the supply table at the back of the room, where I had put out the magazines they would use. I had also put a supply of green construction paper, cut to 8 by 18 inches, on the table.

I said to the children, "When you leave the rug, pick up one sheet of green construction paper and one magazine from the supply table. When you get to your seat, the first thing you need to do is to fold the green paper in half. Then begin your search in the magazine for examples of the shapes. When you cut out a picture that you want to include in your book of cubes, cones, cylinders, and spheres, put it inside your folded green paper. We won't be doing any gluing today. Today your job is to hunt for pictures and cut them out."

When the students were working, I noticed that Danny had cut a picture of a jeep from a magazine. "What shape did you find on a jeep?" I asked him. Because *round* was one of the words on our chart about spheres, I wondered if Danny classified the wheels as spheres.

"The wheels are round," Danny replied, as I had expected.

I responded, "So if the wheels are round, what shape are they? Which shapes that we read about today were round?"

"Well," Danny said, "a cylinder and a sphere are both round, but tires aren't shaped like a ball, they are shaped like a tube. Tires are cylinders, short cylinders." I hadn't thought of tires having a cylindrical shape but indeed they are a "short cylinder," as Danny had put it.

The students were very creative in finding several representations of the four shapes. This activity helped the children make connections between three-dimensional objects and their two-dimensional representations. It also gave them practice with the attributes of each of the four shapes.

Day 2

The following day the students began to organize the pictures they had cut out into four categories: cubes, cones, cylinders, and spheres. "I'd like you to have three to six examples of each solid," I told them. As they did this, I walked around the classroom observing and asking some children to explain which shape a particular item illustrated.

After the children had selected and sorted their shapes, I showed them a piece of white construction paper that I had cut slightly shorter than the green construction paper. "I cut it shorter so that it will fit inside your cover and look neat when you staple your pages," I explained as I modeled how to fold the white paper in half and insert it into the green paper cover. Then I demonstrated how to label their white paper, writing the name of one of the solid shapes on each of the four sections formed by folding. Finally I said, "Now you'll arrange and glue the pictures you cut on the correct pages. When you're done, you'll staple your book together using just two staples." I modeled how to staple the green and white papers to secure the booklet.

The Second Lesson

Day 1

I read *Cubes, Cones, Cylinders, and Spheres* to another class of second graders. From their study of geometry, the students were familiar with the four shapes in Tana Hoban's book and their attributes. Their earlier work had included looking at silhouettes of the solids projected on the overhead, which gave them experience relating two-dimensional and three-dimensional shapes. A chart of geometry vocabulary was posted in the classroom. Because these children had more prior experience than the class to which I taught the previous lesson, I handled the reading of the book differently. If your class isn't as well prepared as this group was, I suggest reading the book in the way I did in the previous lesson and then using this activity in addition to or instead of having the students make their own books.

I brought to the rug the box with the four wooden solids—a cube, a cone, a cylinder, and a sphere. I gathered the students on the rug and said, "You've been learning about geometric shapes and collecting words about them." I motioned toward the chart posted.

Then I showed the children each of the four wooden solids and continued, "These wooden solids help us learn about the attributes of these shapes. Now I want you to think about where in the world around us we see these shapes." I held up the book, read the title, and said, "In this book, you'll see just a few of the ways these shapes present themselves in the world. As I turn the pages, let's not talk. Just look at what's pictured as examples of the shapes."

As I turned the pages, the children silently viewed the photographs. When we reached the end of the book, I said, "Raise your hand if you can think of examples of cubes, cones, cylinders, or spheres that are different from the examples in the book."

Nearly every hand went up, and I gave time for the students to share their ideas.

"A pop can," Jenny began.

Wanting the students to identify both the object and the shape, I asked, "What kind of shape is a pop can?"

"A cylinder," she replied without hesitation.

Troy shared next, "A golf ball is a sphere."

"An apple is like a sphere," Nikita explained. "It is mostly round."

"The tip of a pencil is a cylinder if it is sharpened," Tamari offered.

"A garbage can is a cylinder, but some of them are more like cubes. Well, a rectangle-shaped cube," Logan distinguished.

I said, "Your homework assignment tonight is to collect at least two examples of each shape and bring it to school tomorrow in a grocery bag. All of the items you find must fit into one bag. If something doesn't fit, choose something that's smaller so that all of your items fit. I have a grocery bag for each of you to take home today to help you remember the assignment. Also to help you remember, I need you to record the names of the shapes on your bag. I'll write them on the board for you to copy. I think you should also write your name on your bag so you can tell it apart from everyone else's."

As the students watched, I wrote on the board:

cube

cone

cylinder

sphere

I dismissed the students to return to their seats and write their own names and the names of the shapes on their bags.

At the end of the day, I made sure that all of the children took their bags home. I also took two bags home. In one I placed four items, one for each shape. I used the other bag to collect various items that students could select from if they had been absent or hadn't done the assignment.

Day 2

Before the students arrived the next morning, I wrote on the board, which is the first place children look as they enter the room:

Good Morning! Today is Tuesday, April 4th.

Put your bag on the floor next to your seat.

Do not share what is in your bag.

After our morning meeting we began the activity. The students were very curious about how we were going to use the items in the grocery bags.

"I know that many of you are eager to share the cubes, cones, cylinders, and spheres you found, but we're not going to reveal them just yet. Rather than just show and tell what you brought, you'll each write a riddle about what's in your bag. I've already written my riddles. See if you can guess what's in my bag."

I had written riddles for two objects on overhead transparencies. I projected the first riddle, revealing one clue at a time by using a piece of paper to cover the ones that followed.

I am circular at one end and pointed on the other.
I have a triangle silhouette and a circle silhouette.
You wear me at parties.
What am I? What shape am I?

The students easily guessed a birthday hat or party hat. I pulled the hat from my bag and the room erupted with cheers. I shared the clues for the second riddle I had prepared, again disclosing just one line at a time.

I have two circle faces.
I have a rectangle for my middle.
I wear this on my lips.
What am I? What shape am I?

Again, the clues left little margin for error—the students guessed "lipstick" and "ChapStick."

I then explained, "When you write your riddles, the idea isn't to trick or stump others, but to give good clues that demonstrate your knowledge of the attributes of the solid." I wrote on the board to show the structure of the riddle.

Clue 1
Clue 2
Clue 3
What am I? What shape am I?

The students got to work and I circulated and gave help as needed. Some students rummaged in the bag of extra objects that I had brought. Every student wrote at least two riddles, and some who had found and brought in examples of all four shapes wrote four.

After the students wrote their riddles, I used class time over the next few weeks for them to present their riddles. "Choose just one of your riddles to present," I told them. When presenting, a student would come to the front of the room and read the clues one by one. After reading the last line—What am I? What shape am I?—she or he would call on someone to guess. If the guess was correct, the child would reveal the item from their bag.

Figure 8–1: Kayla's riddle
was about a die.

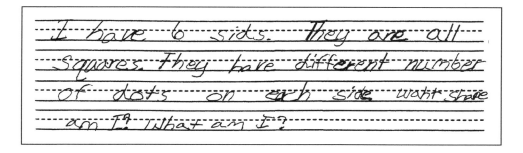

I have 6 sids. They are all
squares. They have different number
of dots on each side. watt shape
am I? What am I?

Figure 8–2: Jon wrote
about a basketball.

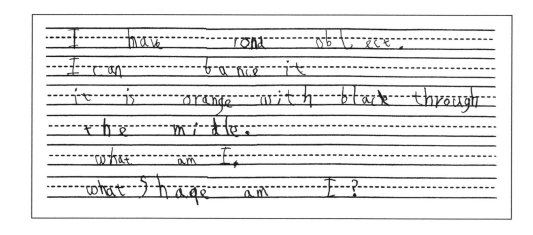

I have rond objece.
I can bance it
it is orange with black through
the midle.
what am I.
what Shape am I?

Figure 8–3: Brett's riddle
about a cylinder-shaped
object stumped the class.

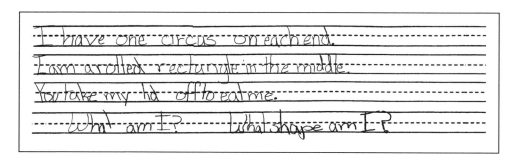

I have one circus on each end.
I am a rolled rectungle in the middle.
You take my hd off to eat me.
what am I? what shape am I?

Kayla's example of a cube was a die while Jon wrote about a basketball being a sphere. (See Figures 8–1 and 8–2.)

Brett's riddle about a potato chip can stumped the class, but not because the clues were misleading or inaccurate. (See Figure 8–3.) The students knew the shape was a cylinder, but they had to stop and think about what type of food came in a cylindrical container.

How Tall, How Short, How Faraway

In *How Tall, How Short, How Faraway* (1999), David Adler helps students learn how ancient Egyptians and Romans used their fingers, hands, arms, and legs as tools for measuring length. The informative text introduces nonstandard measures—digits, palms, spans, cubits, and paces—and explains the difference between the U.S. and metric systems of standard measures. Throughout the book, Adler prompts readers to measure various lengths and distances.

The lesson based on this book engages second graders in measuring with nonstandard units, giving them a foundation that will later help them understand the usefulness of standard measures.

MATERIALS

***Measuring in the Classroom* worksheet**, 1 per student (see Blackline Masters)

Day 1

Introducing the Investigation

Before reading *How Tall, How Short, How Faraway* to a class of second graders, I said to the children, "People have been measuring lengths of things for thousands of years to find out how tall or short or faraway they are. What do you think people might have used to measure lengths?"

Joshua shared his idea first: "They might have used their feet for how big they take a step—well, just a normal step like this." He quickly got up and demonstrated. "From this foot to this foot," he said, posing so we could see his step.

"Right," I commented. "What Joshua has just demonstrated is called a *step*."

"Maybe they used their hands?" asked Kayla, unsure of her idea.

"Yes, they did use their hands," I replied. "The people who lived in Egypt used their hands to measure in several ways." Before going further I pulled down the world map and said, "Let's find where Egypt is on the map." I gave a clue—that Egypt is in northern Africa—and chose two students to come up and find it on the map. Then I chose another pair of students to come up and show where the United States is located. A third pair of students used our globe to point to both Egypt and the United States. I thanked the children and continued.

"Thousands of years ago in the country of Egypt," I said, pointing to Egypt on the map, "people measured with their hands like this." I held my hand up with my fingers together and asked the students to do the same. "The width of my four fingers, from my pinky to my pointer finger, was called a palm." Then I asked the children to spread all five fingers apart and said, "Now you're showing a span. The distance from your thumb to your pinky is called a span. These ways of measuring lengths, and more, are explained in this book *How Tall, How Short, How Faraway*."

I showed the children the cover of the book, then read aloud. I began, "In ancient Egypt, fingers, hands, and arms were used as measuring tools. The width of one finger was a digit." I held up an index finger and many of the students did too. As I continued reading about palms, spans, and cubits, the students held up their hands or arms to show each measurement as it was introduced.

After asking the students to use their hands and arms to measure their heights, the book introduces the *pace*. I read, "Every two steps is a pace, a measure used in ancient Rome."

The next two pages relate a conversation about the Coliseum. Three people are debating just how far away the Coliseum is in terms of miles and paces. As I read the text aloud, we revisited the wall map to locate where Rome is today. I commented that the Coliseum still stands. The children were amazed. Later that day one of the students checked out a book on Rome from the media center and we were able to get a look at the Coliseum as it may have looked in ancient times and as it is now.

How Tall, How Short, How Faraway addresses the problem of nonstandard units resulting in different measurements for the same objects, then introduces the idea of using standard units. It explains that the system we use in the United States is based on Roman measures. The book also introduces the metric units of length, explaining that the metric system was first proposed more than three hundred years ago by a French priest, Father Gabriel Mouton. Several real-world measuring problems are included for readers to do with the models of 8-inch and 20-centimeter rulers in the book.

This book is an effective introduction for many possible classroom measuring activities. For this lesson I drew from the information presented at the beginning of the book and engaged the children in measuring with their hand spans, palms, and digits. I wanted to give them experience measuring lengths using their own hand measurements as a basis for later helping them learn about the usefulness of standard measures.

"Today we'll use our hands to measure just as the people of Egypt used their hands long, long ago," I began. "In what ways could we use hands to measure the length of our world map?"

"We could put our fingers together like this," said Stuart, "but I forgot what it was called."

"A palm," whispered Vladimir.

"OK," I said and on the board traced the outline of my four fingers held tightly together. Next to the outline I wrote *palm*.

"What other ways could we measure with our hands?"

"We could spread our hands out," Christina said.

As I traced my open hand on the board I asked, "Do you remember what this measurement is called?"

"Span," replied several students. I wrote *span* next to the outline of my open hand.

"Is there any other way we could use our hands to measure?" I asked.

"A digit," suggested Stephanie, holding up her index finger.

I traced my index finger on the board and labeled it *digit*.

"Whisper which one of these measurements is the longest," I encouraged.

"Span," whispered the class.

I continued, "Today we are going to use these three ways to measure the lengths of things around our classroom. We need to make wise decisions about which measurement is best to use when we start to measure, spans, palms, or digits." I demonstrated each measurement with my hand as I mentioned it. Then I turned to the board and drew a chart like the one on the worksheet they would use for recording. (See page 54 and Blackline Masters.)

Referring to the pull-down map, I said, "Let's think about measuring the length of our map with our hands." I wrote *map* on the chart at the top of the first column and continued, "Because the map is big, I think we should use the longest measure that we have. Show me with your hand which hand measure you would start with to measure something this long." The students held up their open hands to show that they would use their spans.

"How we would use a span to measure this? Where would we begin?" I asked.

Measuring in the Classroom

Object	Span	Palm	Digit

"At one end and go to the other," said some students. Others pointed to the left corner of the map.

"Like this?" I asked, placing my left span with my pinky at the map's corner. The children nodded their agreement. I continued measuring with my spans but intentionally left big gaps between where I placed my open hands.

Some children giggled while others protested: "No." "That's not right." "They have to touch." "Don't skip so much."

"How should I measure?" I asked.

"You shouldn't leave spaces between your hands," Miriam said.

"Your fingers need to touch each time you move your hand," Benjamin added.

"Could someone come up and show us how you would measure this map using spans?" I asked. I called on Akyme. While he was coming up to the map, I said, "The rest of you can help by counting the spans as Akyme measures."

Akyme carefully demonstrated how to measure with his spans while the other students counted. I commented on how he placed his open hands carefully, making sure that his fingers just touched so there weren't spaces between his spans. When Akyme got near the end of the map, there was some space yet to measure but not a full span. I instructed him to hold his last span in place as I recorded *16* on our chart to show the children where they would enter the number of spans they counted when they did their own measurements.

"What hand measurement could fit in the leftover space at the end?" I asked.

"It looks like we could fit at least one palm," Neil predicted.

"So should we try a palm?" I asked.

"Yes," the children chorused.

Akyme placed a closed palm next to his last span. There was still space left between his palm and the end of the map, but it was clear that another palm wouldn't fit. I recorded *1* under the palm column on the chart while Akyme completed measuring with his digits. Two digits fit, and I entered *2* in the digit column to complete recording the measurement of the map.

Object	Span	Palm	Digit
map	15	1	2

Next I showed the students the worksheet they would be using. I explained, "You'll work with a partner and you'll both measure the same five items in the classroom. What do you think would be good things in the room to measure with our spans, palms, and digits?" We looked around the classroom and brainstormed objects they might measure. After this discussion, I set the limits of what they could choose—nothing shorter than a new crayon or longer than the area rug they were sitting on.

I further clarified what they were to do: "You and your partner will each complete your own chart, even though you're measuring the same things. But do the measurements together, each helping the other the way we helped Akyme. For each object, record how many of each measure you used. After you've measured all five objects, then you each answer the question at the bottom of your own worksheet. It says, 'Were your measurements the same as your partners? Why or why not?'" I pointed to the questions on a worksheet. "Do you have any questions about what you are to do before you get started?"

Observing the Students

There were no questions so I organized the students into pairs. As they began to work the room was filled with enthusiastic activity. The students were excited about using their own hands to measure and enjoyed the freedom of choosing what they would measure. As they worked, I circulated around the room observing.

Lily and Stephanie worked together. On her worksheet, Stephanie explained why their measurements weren't the same. She wrote: *They where different because my partner had smaller hands.* (See Figure 9–1.) Lily didn't explain why their measurements were different, but simply stated, *thay were biger.* (See Figure 9–2.)

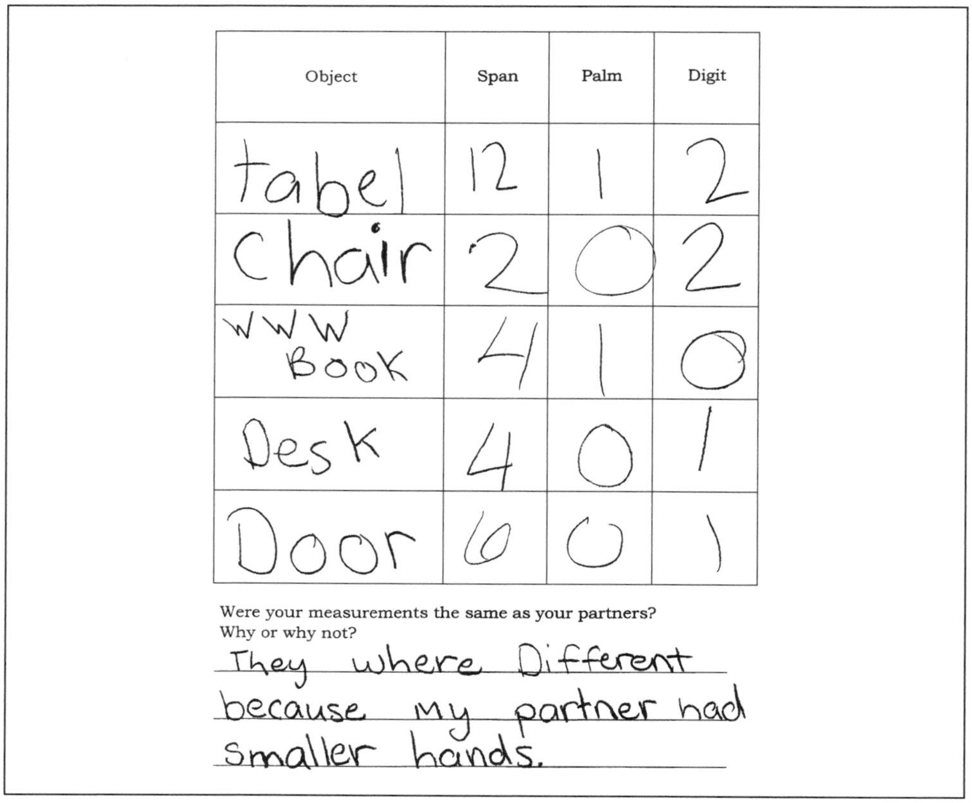

Figure 9–1: Stephanie explained why her measurements differed from Lily's.

Object	Span	Palm	Digit
tabel	12	1	2
chair	2	0	2
www Book	4	1	0
Desk	4	0	1
Door	6	0	1

Were your measurements the same as your partners? Why or why not?

They where Different because my partner had smaller hands.

Math and Nonfiction, Grades K–2

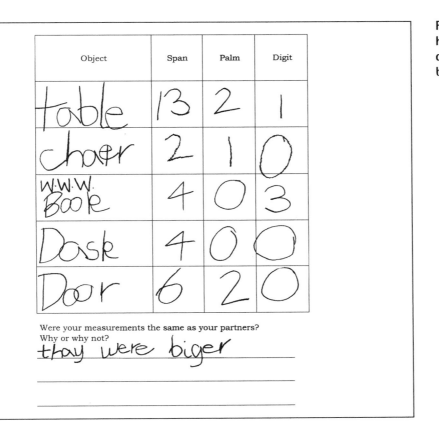

Object	Span	Palm	Digit
table	13	2	1
chaer	2	1	0
W.W.W. Book	4	0	3
Dosk	4	0	0
Door	6	2	0

Were your measurements the same as your partners?
Why or why not?
thay were biger

Jasmine, Jeffrey, and Marin didn't work together but their answers to the question at the bottom of the worksheet were typical of the answers I received from the others in the class. (See Figures 9–3, 9–4, and 9–5 on the following pages.)

Day 2

The following day I opened with a question: "Yesterday many of you explained that your measurements weren't the same even though you had measured the same five objects. Why was this so?" We discussed this together.

Follow-up Lessons

I saved the students' papers for a later lesson in which I returned to the book, reread the part about the need for standard measures, and introduced the children to using rulers. They measured their same five objects using feet and inches instead of spans, palms, and digits. Later in the year, I introduced them to metric measures of length.

How Tall, How Short, How Faraway

Figure 9–3: Jasmine noted that her hands weren't the same size as her partner's.

Object	Span	Palm	Digit
Map	13	0	1
Door	7	0	1
Tabel	14	0	1
Book	0	3	2
Clipbord	1	1	1

Were your measurements the same as your partners? Why or why not?

Some were the same.
Some were't the same.
because are hand arnt the
same.

Figure 9–4: Jeffrey's hands were a different length than his partner's.

Object	Span	Palm	Digit
clock	2	0	0
tabol	12	1	1
Paint shirt	5	0	1
Paper	2	0	0
carpet	14	0	1

Were your measurements the same as your partners? Why or why not?

no. are hands are
diffrint lanths.

Object	Span	Palm	Digit
Bord	11	1	Zewow
Book	2	1	Zewow
thermometer	5	Zewow	Zewow
Lockr	12	1	Zewow
Witboord	23	1	Zewow

Were your measurements the same as your partners?
Why or why not?

NO my partners hand is smolr.

Figure 9–5: Marin's hand was bigger than her partner's.

More Than One

Miriam Schlein's *More Than One* (1996) introduces the concept that one unit can be made up of more than one thing. *One pair* is always two, *one week* is seven days, *one baseball team* is nine players, and *one dozen* is twelve. *One family* can be two, three, four, five, six, or more people. One can also mean "a lot," as in *one forest* has a lot of trees or *one flock* has a lot of birds.

In the lesson using this book, first and second graders use mathematical language to describe a self-portrait, applying the concept that *one* can be an exact number or can describe a variable number of things.

MATERIALS

hand-held mirrors, 1 per group of students, or 1 full-length mirror

Miriam Schlein's *More Than One* is ideal for introducing children to the idea that *one* doesn't always mean *just* one. *More Than One* explains how the number one can refer to a single item but can also be used to portray groups: two shoes in a pair, seven days in a week, twelve eggs in a dozen. One can also describe groups where the number in each group can vary or be hard to determine, such as the number of people in one family, the number of birds in one flock, or the number of fish in one school.

I gathered the first- and second-grade students on the rug to read *More Than One* aloud to them. They enjoyed the simple text. When I finished reading, I asked, "What did you learn about the number one from this book?"

"The book explained that one can mean one like one sun in the sky, but sometimes it means more than one," Brock offered.

"One can mean a really, really, really big number like a million, billion, or trillion," Amanda stressed, "like sand. One beach has so much sand we can't even count it all, but all the sand put together is just one beach."

"The book showed that one can mean nine. Like in baseball, nine players make a team like the picture in the book showed. But one team can also mean five, like a basketball team, and a football team has eleven players on the field at once or else they get a penalty," explained Mark, an avid sports fan.

"So, I've heard you say that one can refer to one exact thing, but one can also refer to groups that have more than just one in them." On the board I wrote *more than one* and under it I created a two-column chart, titling the columns *exact number* and *variable number*. Although *variable* wasn't a term that the students were familiar with, I introduced it by simply using it throughout the lesson along with more familiar language like the word "changeable." I've found that by exposing young learners to mathematical terminology early, most begin to use the vocabulary correctly to describe their thinking.

"What were some of the ideas presented in the book about the number one that we could list in our *exact number* column?" I asked.

Meagan began with some uncertainty: "I think *pair* would go there."

"You're right," I confirmed. I recorded the word *pair* under the heading *exact number* on the chart and asked, "Can you explain why you thought that, Meagan?"

"Well, like a pair of shoes is two, but it's one pair of shoes," she said, more confidently now.

"One dozen always means twelve, like a dozen doughnuts— yummy," said Jasmine. I added *dozen* to the first column in the list.

"One week is always seven days, so *week* should go under exact numbers," Sari directed. I wrote *week* in the first column.

"Are there any other ideas you can remember from the book that mean an exact number each time?" I asked.

"I think *team* would go there even though it changes like Mark said, because it's still an exact number," Eric thought. I understood what Eric was trying to explain and saw that a few other classmates shared his reasoning. I asked Sammy to explain further.

"It's like one team is an exact number, like nine players on a baseball team," she shared. "But if you're talking about another team, like a volleyball team, then the number would be six, so one team is six players."

"I think *team* would go on the *various* side because it is like family, it depends on what kind," Julian said. I didn't correct Julian's mispronouncing *variable*. *Various* is a word that Julian was familiar with, and I felt confident that he would make the shift after hearing *variable* used more often.

Others agreed with Julian's reasoning, so I wrote *team* under both the *exact number* and *variable numbers* columns.

"What else can I write in the variable number column?" I asked. "How was the number one used in the book to describe groups with changing numbers?" I recorded as the children reported. Soon our list looked like this:

More than one...

exact numbers	variable numbers
pair	team
dozen	family
week	flock
team	ocean
	forest
	beach
	crowd
	school

Then I introduced the activity of drawing self-portraits and writing about them using the mathematical idea that one is one but can also be more than one. I said, "So the book *More Than One* showed us how *one* can mean more than one. For example, we are *one class,* but within this class are twenty-six students."

"And one teacher," corrected Roy.

"So all of us together, the twenty-six of you plus me, make up one class," I continued. "I'd like you to begin thinking about the one *you* that helps make up our one class. Today we are going to create self-portraits and describe them using some of the mathematical ideas presented in the book. For example, let's just focus on our faces."

The students were still sitting cross-legged on the floor facing me. I asked them to turn so they were knee-to-knee with the person sitting next to them. "Study your partner's face. How many eyes do they have?"

"Two," chorused the class.

"How many *pairs* of eyes do they have?" I emphasized by pointing to *pair* on our chart.

"One," the students replied easily.

I continued inquiring, asking about the number of ears and number of pairs of ears, and then about noses and nostrils, mouths and lips.

I moved on to include the variable numbers. I began, "So we have many pairs on our face. We have a pair of eyes, ears, nostrils, and lips. Now everyone smile a big toothy smile at your partner. How many smiles do you each have?"

"One," the students replied, giggling at their classmates' goofy grins.

"How many teeth are in that smile? I want you each to count your own teeth using your tongue and then open up and have your partner check your count just like a dentist might look into your mouth." The students were a little silly during this activity but it was worthwhile because it generated a set of numbers that varied because some of their smiles were missing teeth.

Giovanna was determined to describe her smile using a fractional part. She explained, "I have a smile with nineteen and a half teeth because I lost this one and now I have a big tooth coming in, but it is only halfway in. See?" She smiled and turned her head for all to take note, then added, "So I have nineteen teeth plus this half tooth." I could see many of the students begin to recount their teeth with their tongues to determine if they too could count a tooth that was just partly showing.

"So we each have one mouth or smile with one set of teeth, but the number of teeth that makes up that smile or set can be different. Some of you have twenty-four teeth, some have twenty-five and a half, and others have twenty-six. The number of teeth varies," I said, pointing to the heading *Variable number* on the board, "but the number of mouths on each face is still just one."

We talked about the tops of our heads and the hairs on them being too many to count, like the trees in the forest and the birds in the flock we had seen in the book's illustrations.

I asked the students to turn and face me. I told them once more that they were going to be drawing portraits of themselves. "Then you'll write at least five mathematical statements that describe your face," I said. For those students who needed an extra mathematical challenge or who enjoyed drawing, I suggested, "Or you can draw your entire body and include additional facts about *one* part. For example, you have one hand but five fingers."

I made mirrors available to students—a full-length mirror, which I borrowed from the kindergarten room, and several hand mirrors. Some students thoroughly enjoyed using the mirrors and studied themselves carefully before they got started and as they drew. Others drew their portraits without so much as a glance in the mirror.

I instructed the students to use pencil first for their drawing and writing. They could add color once their pencil drawings and their mathematical descriptions were complete.

A sentence starter is always helpful for some students. I listed some prompts on the board for them to record on their papers and think about:

I have two ____ *but just one* ____.
I have five ____ *but just one* ____.
I have lots of ____ *but just one* ____.

The idea of "more than one" is depicted in Figures 10–1, 10–2, and 10–3. Joe and Morgan's drawings both show eyelashes. Each chose to handle this number in different manners. Joe used an exact number *4*

Figure 10–1: Joe worked diligently to complete his illustration. The concept of "more than one" came easily to him but expressing it in writing proved more challenging.

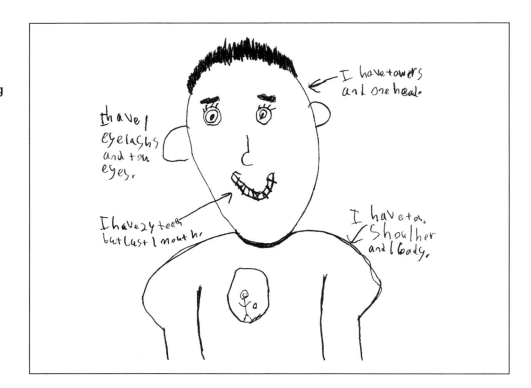

Figure 10–2: Morgan's labels surrounded her self-portrait.

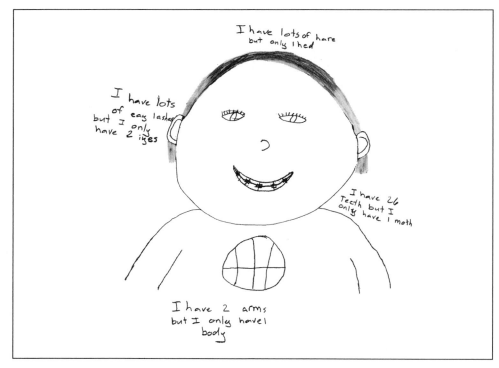

and then was sure that his drawing matched that number. Morgan was comfortable using an approximation, stating that she had *lots of eay lashes,* a statement that accurately describes her drawing.

Rachel relied heavily on the sentence starters. She wrote, *I have ten fingers but only two hands,* although the self-portrait is of her face and not her entire body.

I have Lots of hair but only one head.
I have two lips but only one mouth
I have ten fingers but only two hands

I have two nostrols but only one nose

Figure 10–3: Rachel put her labels at the top and bottom of her drawing.

After the students had completed their self-portraits, I collected the pictures and hung them all together in the hallway. Next to them I posted a large sheet of paper on which I had recorded two questions taken from the book, leaving space beneath each question to record answers.

Can one be more than one?

Can one be different, different every time?

I took the students into the hall the following day and gave them the opportunity to talk about their drawings and what they wrote. I asked them to answer the first question I had written: "Can one be more than one?"

"Yes," they replied together. I wrote *Yes*.

I read the next question: "Can one be different, different every time?"

Again the students replied easily: "Yes."

I wrote: *Yes, one can be twenty-six kids in a class. How many are in your class?* I hoped this last question would prompt readers of our display to think about the mathematical idea being presented. Over the next week, many classes stopped outside of our room to answer the questions and take note of the mathematical concepts the students had illustrated in their drawings.

My Map Book

Turn a page in Sara Fanelli's *My Map Book* (1995) and you'll reveal a new two-page map of something important in a child's life: Map of My Day, Map of My Neighborhood, Map of My Face, Map of My Bedroom, and more. Each of the twelve maps includes unique details, and the colorful artwork suggests the artwork of a young child.

In this lesson, second-grade students draw maps of their classroom, which engages them informally with scale and helps develop their spatial awareness.

MATERIALS

white drawing paper (9-by-12 inches if your classroom is rectangular; 9-by-9 inches if it is more square than rectangular), 1 sheet per student

12-inch rulers, 1 per student

Before reading *My Map Book* to a class of second graders, I pulled down the classroom map of the United States and asked, "Why do we need maps?" A few students raised their hands, and I waited for more to do so. I called on Arianna.

"We need maps to tell us where things are," she said.

"Maps show us which direction to go to get somewhere so we don't get lost," Bruce added.

"They're like a drawing of what's around you. And they show where you are and what things you are close to," Shira said.

"We need maps to show us where the oceans are and where the mountains are and where you live," Tuong said.

"So maps help us find our way around," I summarized. "In this book, you will see some really unusual maps that do exactly that."

I shared the book with the students, being sure to spend enough time on each two-page spread for the children to explore the entire map and all its clever details. On the Treasure Map, the first in the book, the students were fascinated by the monster, the two guardians of the treasure, the knights on horseback, and the buildings. This map is followed by the Map of My Bedroom, which shows two beds, a desk, a small carpet, slippers, and more. The Map of My Family presents a simple family tree. The Map of My Day lays out a day from morning to the dreams at night that follow story time. The other maps in the book are titled Map of My Tummy, Color Map, Map of My Neighborhood, Map of My Heart, Map of My Dog, Road Map, Map of My Face, and Map of the Seaside. The book presents a unique and unexpected view of the world, and the children were amused and surprised the entire way through.

"Today we are going to create maps of our classroom," I told the students. I showed them a few of the pages in the book that would be helpful for the task. First we looked at the Map of My Bedroom. Because we have windows along one wall in our classroom, I pointed out how the windows in the book are drawn flat even though real windows go up and have height. I also talked about the different sizes of the furniture in the bedroom. "Which child do you think is younger?" I asked, pointing to the two different size beds in the illustration. This led to a discussion about furniture size and accurate representation. We talked about how the student desks and chairs in our classroom are the same size and should therefore be the same size on their maps, and about which furniture is larger than the student desks and should be shown larger on their maps.

"Your desk will be bigger," Nick said, commenting on my teacher desk.

"Yeah, your desk is about two of ours," Cam responded matter-of-factly.

Jarvis said, "The tables are bigger."

"And the rug that we are sitting on would be biggest of all," Ellie noted.

I turned to the Map of My Neighborhood to discuss perspective and the shapes of the objects that would be included on their maps of our classroom. We talked about how the house in the book's map is shaped like a square and how the playground is an irregular shape with six sides. The children were familiar with the term *hexagon* for a six-sided shape. "How many sides does a hexagon have?" I asked.

"Six," the children responded in unison.

"Will our table look like this playground when you draw it?" I asked.

"No, the playground is kind of squishy shaped and long," Melanie volunteered, pointing to the picture in the book. "Our table is perfect shaped."

"Tell me what you mean by 'perfect shaped,'" I probed.

After some thought, Melanie said, "Well, it . . . the sides are all the same."

I called on Stanley, who said, "The hexagon table will be a lot smaller than the playground. The playground takes up almost the whole page. Well, it's half of the map, but this whole side." He pointed to the playground in the illustration as Melanie had done.

Holding up a piece of 9-by-12-inch white drawing paper and a ruler, I instructed, "Use pencil to draw your map of our classroom. Using pencil makes it easier for you to make corrections or change your mind about something. Also, it's good to use a ruler to help you draw straight lines. After you label the objects on your map, if you'd like to you can add color with construction paper scraps, crayons, and markers."

I asked if the students had questions about the maps they were going to create. Marne raised her hand. "Do we have to include every part of the room or can we just draw one part of the classroom?"

"It's fine for you to focus on just part of the room," I responded. "You can draw a map of just this half that we're seated in, or that half, or the corner where my table is. Or you can draw a map of the entire room, just as the author of this book has done."

Shelby had a question, "Can we draw a map of our desks?"

"You mean the inside of your desk?" I clarified. Shelby nodded.

I thought about the lesson's purpose and decided that this would be fine. "That's OK, too," I responded.

I distributed pieces of drawing paper and rulers and the students got right to work. All the children drew their maps without taking formal measurements of anything in the room. A few folded their pieces of paper into halves or fourths. When I asked Michael why he had folded his paper, he said, "Well, you see, it helps me know where to begin and where the middle is."

"Where the middle of the room is?" I asked, seeing that his drawing was of only a corner of the room. (See Figure 11–1.)

"No," he responded, "the middle of my paper, so then I have an idea of where to put things in my map."

Michael's explanation helped me understand that he was trying to be accurate in placing items on his map. Although the objects in his drawing are placed correctly, they are out of scale.

Payten used a die to check the size of the student desks in her drawing. (See Figure 11–2.) Drawing one square at a time, she placed the die inside each square to check its size so that all twenty-nine desks would be about the same.

Shelby drew a map of the inside of her desk. It showed how she used space and organized her materials. (See Figure 11–3.)

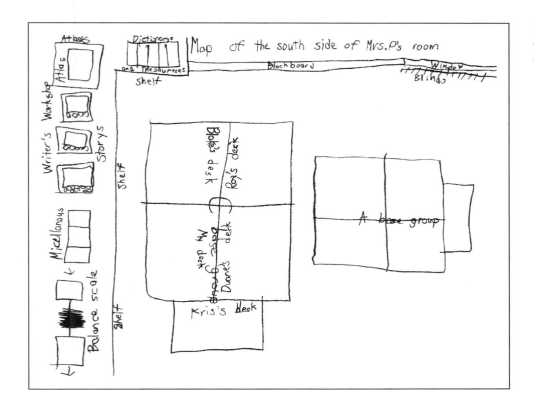

Figure 11–1: Michael drew one corner of the classroom.

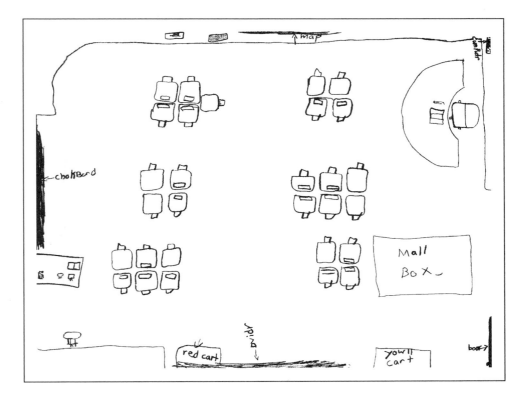

Figure 11–2: Payten drew the entire room, using a die as a template for the desks.

Figure 11–3: Shelby mapped the inside of her desk.

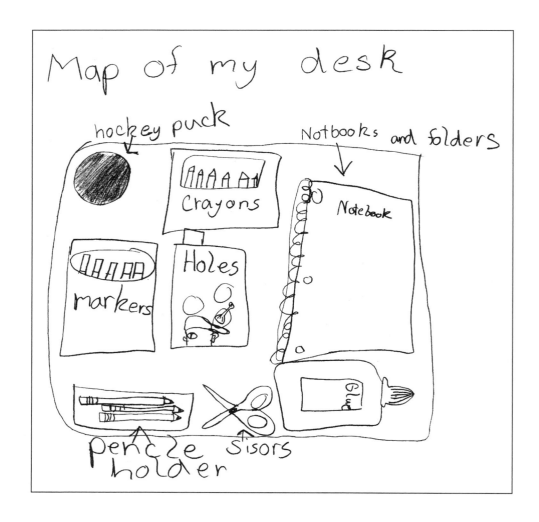

Math and Nonfiction, Grades K–2

Roman Numerals I to MM

In *Roman Numerals I to MM: Numerabilia Romana Uno ad Duo Mila* (1996), Arthur Geisert cleverly teaches Roman numerals using illustrations of pigs. First the seven Roman numerals—I, V, X, L, C, D, and M—are presented, each matched to the correct number of pigs. The book then explains how to combine these seven numerals to make the other numbers, again using pigs as examples. At the end of the book, several pages of illustrations present a search-and-count game. The objects in each illustration are named below it with the number of how many there are shown in Roman numerals—IX ducks in a pond, VI clouds, XVI gopher holes, and so on.

In the lesson, second graders learn to play the *Roman Numeral Game,* which familiarizes them with reading and valuing Roman numerals from I to XX.

MATERIALS

20 3-by-5-inch index cards numbered from 1 to 20, with the 6 and 9 underlined to distinguish between them

additional 3-by-5-inch index cards, 20 per pair of students

***The Roman Numeral Game* rules,** 1 copy per pair of students (see Blackline Masters)

With the second graders gathered around me, I asked, "Where have you seen Roman numerals used?" Many hands went up.

"In the Superbowl it says Superbowl XXXII or something," Randal offered, saying the *X*s and *I*s, not the number thirty-two.

"You see Roman numerals on clocks," Whitney contributed.

"Sometimes books have Roman numbers in them instead of regular numbers," Rylie said.

As the students offered their ideas, I recorded them on the board. After all the children had shared, I asked, "Who knows another place where you've seen Roman numerals?"

Preston said, "The Olympics have Roman numerals to tell how many times they've had them."

"There are Roman numerals on my church," said Eric.

"I've seen them on my dad's office building," Samantha chimed in.

No other hands were up. I said, "If you think of some other places you see Roman numerals in your life, we'll add them to our list later. Right now, I'm going to read a book to you that will help you understand how to read and write Roman numerals. And I think you'll really enjoy the illustrations."

The book begins by presenting the seven letters that stand for Roman numerals—I, V, X, L, C, D, and M. On each of the next seven pages, the number represented by one of the letters is illustrated with the corresponding number of pigs. The students giggled at Geisert's funny illustrations, especially the one that shows pigs on seesaws. On the pages for I, V, X, and L, the children quietly and spontaneously counted the number of pigs represented by the numerals.

The book next describes how to read Roman numerals when the same letters are placed side-by-side two or three times—II, XX, CC, III, XXX, and CCC—again illustrating with pigs. The author explains that we don't put V, L, or D side-by-side with itself because when two of them are together, they add up to a number that is represented by its own letter—VV = X, LL = C, and DD = M. M, the largest Roman numeral, can be used as many times in a row as you like. Then the book introduces the rules for adding and subtracting so that children can make sense of Roman numerals like IV and VI.

Pages XVIII through XXI show the Roman numerals from I to XX, each with the corresponding number of pigs. I allowed time for the students to read each numeral and count the number of pigs.

The last section of the book presents search-and-count illustrations. Beneath each is a list of the objects that are in it and a notation of how many of each there are: IX ducks in a pond, VI clouds, XVI gopher holes, and so on. I didn't show these pages to the class at this time. I planned to make the book available to the children to reread on their own during the week; they could tackle the puzzles then, if they wished.

"What letters are used for Roman numerals?" I asked. As the children volunteered letters, I wrote them on the board, listing them in order of value, although the students didn't offer them in order. I reread the first six pages of the book, then added the values of the letters to my list on the board:

Roman Numerals

$$I = 1$$
$$V = 5$$
$$X = 10$$
$$L = 50$$
$$C = 100$$
$$D = 500$$
$$M = 1,000$$

"Do you notice any patterns in our list?" Some children had anticipated my question and their hands were flapping wildly.

Jennifer stated, "I notice that it goes one, five, one, five, one, and five."

"Tell me more," I prompted.

"Well, first there is one and then five, and then a one again but in the tens spot, so it's one ten and then five so it's fifty, and it keeps going like that to one thousand," Jennifer clarified.

"Can anyone else describe the pattern?" I asked.

"It's a growing pattern," Jon said.

"It's true that it's a growing pattern," I responded. "How is it growing?"

Tuan came up to the board and explained, pointing to the numbers as he spoke. "Starting with one you add four to get five and then add five to get ten. Then you add *forty*," Tuan said, emphasizing the first syllable in forty, "to get fifty and then add fifty to get one hundred. Then just keep going, add four hundred to get five hundred and then add five hundred to get a thousand." Each time Tuan mentioned the number he was adding, he emphasized the words *four* and *five*.

I asked if anyone could explain Tuan's pattern using number sentences. Veronica and Ellie volunteered. They came to the board and wrote:

$$1 + 4 = 5$$
$$5 + 5 = 10$$
$$10 + 40 = 50$$
$$50 + 50 = 100$$
$$100 + 400 = 500$$
$$500 + 500 = 1,000$$

After the girls had finished I recapped by underlining the 4s and 5s in the second addends of each sentence to illustrate the pattern that Tuan had described.

Then I said, "Today we're going to play a game that will help you learn how to read, write, and name the values of Roman numerals. We're going to focus on the Roman numerals for the numbers from one to twenty."

To introduce the game, I asked the students to sit in one large circle. This gave them a moment to stretch while they got into the configuration for the next part of the lesson. I distributed twenty 3-by-5-inch index cards, each with a numeral from 1 through 20 written neatly on one side, going around the circle so that the cards were in consecutive order. Because I had more than twenty students, I asked some to share their cards with a student sitting next to them.

I said, "To play our game today we are going to need playing cards, which is what you're holding in your hands now. Each of you, with some of you working in pairs, has a card with a number on it. As we look again at the pages that show the Roman numerals for the numbers from one through twenty, you'll write the corresponding Roman numeral on the back of your card." With that, I handed a marker to the person holding the card with a one on it. As we looked in the book at the Roman numerals for the numbers from 1 to 20, the students carefully passed the marker around the circle, writing the correct Roman numeral to the blank side of each card. When we had finished, I had all students flip their cards to the side with Arabic numbers.

"Why did I underline the six and the nine on the cards?" I asked.

"So you know which is which," Jamilla said. The others agreed.

"Now flip your card to show the Roman numeral," I instructed. When the children had done so, I asked, "Is there any Roman numeral that might be confused for another if the card were flipped upside-down?"

The students began to flip their cards and soon discovered that IX and XI could be confused, so the children with those cards underlined their numerals to show which way was right side up.

I collected all of the cards, moved to the middle of the circle, and asked Roberto to help me demonstrate how the game is played. Some students scooted in close while other stood behind them in what we call a huddle formation.

"This is called *The Roman Numeral Game*. You'll play it in pairs," I said. I showed the class the rules I had duplicated and read the first rule: "Spread all the cards out in front of both of you. It doesn't matter which side of a card is facing up." I handed Roberto some of the cards and together we spread them out randomly in the middle of the circle, some with the Roman numeral showing and others with the Arabic numeral showing.

I continued, "Rule number two says 'Take turns. On your turn, point to a card, name the numeral on the other side, and then flip the card over to check. If you are correct, the card is yours. If you are not correct, leave the card in the center of the playing area.'"

"I don't get it," Eric said.

"Watch us play for a moment," I said. Then I turned to Roberto and asked, "Do you want to go first or should I?"

"You go," Roberto said.

"OK," I responded. I pointed to the card with VIII on it and ventured, "I think that the numeral on the other side is an eight." I flipped the card over to reveal that I was correct. "So I get to keep this card," I said, moving it to my side. "Now it's your turn."

Roberto pointed to the card with the Arabic numeral 10 showing. "I think X is on the other side," he said, pronouncing the letter X rather than the word *ten*. He checked, grinned, and took the card.

Before I took my next turn, I checked with Eric to see if he was still confused. "I get it now," he said.

Next I deliberately made an error. I pointed to the card with XIV on it and said, "I know that X is ten, and I is one, and V is five, so I think the number is sixteen." A few children gasped. I turned over the card and revealed the numeral fourteen.

Sally said, "You forgot that the I in front of the V means it's four, not six. You goofed."

"So I did," I said. "That means I have to leave this card in the middle. Roberto, now it's your turn."

Roberto took his turn and then we each took one more turn. I stopped to read the last rule: "After all cards have been collected, the winner is the player with the most cards."

I felt confident that the students understood how to play, so rather than finishing the game with Roberto, I grouped the class into pairs so that they could get started. I gave each pair twenty blank index cards and a copy of the rules. "First you'll have to create your cards," I said. "Write the numbers in pencil first, and then check with me or another pair of students to be sure that they're correct. Then you can trace the numerals with markers." The students got busy and the classroom gradually went from a quiet hum to an active buzz as they became involved with playing.

The Roman Numeral Game continued to be popular in our classroom. The students' learning went far beyond my initial objectives of familiarizing them with the Roman numeral system. From playing the extension version of the game, they applied a variety of addition strategies such as looking for groups of ten and using doubles as they computed the total value of their cards.

So You Want to Be President?

So You Want to Be President? (2000) is the 2001 Caldecott Medal winner. Although this book received its honor for David Small's humorous, beautiful, and sometimes mischievous pictures, Judith St. George's text is equally deserving of recognition. The book presents a variety of factual information about our nation's first forty-one presidents in sometimes serious, sometimes silly, and always cleverly illustrated ways.

In this lesson, second graders collect data about jobs they would like to have when they grow up. Working in groups of four, they organize their data in more than one way, then choose one way to record on a graph. They then make generalizations about the graph.

MATERIALS

11 3-by-5-inch sticky notes, each labeled with one job: lawyer, teacher, farmer, sailor, engineer, surveyor, mayor, governor, congressman, senator, ambassador

3-by-5-inch unlined index cards, 3 per student

chart paper, 1 sheet per group of four students

I gathered my class of second graders on the rug to read *So You Want to Be President?* I said, "In the book I'm going to read to you today, you'll learn many fun facts about our country's presidents. How many of you have ever thought of becoming president of the United States?"

More than half of the students raised their hands. I continued, "Well, all of our presidents had other jobs before becoming president, and this book reveals some of those jobs. After we read the book, we'll collect data about the careers that interest you. For a moment, imagine yourself as an adult and think about what job you would enjoy doing."

I paused for a quiet moment and then said, "I'll start reading the book now, and I'll ask you to think about my question after we enjoy the book together." I showed the students the cover of the book. They started to whisper about the cover and a few giggled at the funny caricatures of the presidents.

"It's like Mount Rushmore!" Brandon called out. Several others who had visited the famous monument agreed.

"There are good things about being President and there are bad things about being President," I read from the first page. The next several pages point out good things—for example, living in the White House and enjoying the swimming pool, bowling alley, and movie theater—and bad things—for example, always having to be dressed up. The book presents data about past presidents in various categories, including first names (there were six Jameses, four Johns, four Williams, two Georges, two Andrews, and two Franklins), heights and weights (William Howard Taft weighed more than 300 pounds and had a special tub built in his White House bathroom), ages when elected, number of siblings (Benjamin Harrison had the most—eleven brothers and sisters), pets that have lived in the White House (Theodore Roosevelt's children ran a zoo!), whether or not they had attended college (nine didn't), who had been vice president first, what job they had before becoming president, and more.

After reading the book through once, I went back to the pages that contain data about what our nation's presidents did before becoming leader of the United States. I read, "Almost any job can lead to the White House. Presidents have been lawyers, teachers, farmers, sailors, engineers, surveyors, mayors, governors, congressmen, senators, and ambassadors."

I took the eleven sticky notes on which I had written these jobs and placed them on the board behind me so that all the students could see them. "We have eleven pieces of data here," I said, then read the occupations aloud. Some of the students weren't familiar with a few of them, so I explained. Then I asked, "How could we put the data into categories of jobs that go together in some way?"

After a few moments, Erica raised her hand. She said, "We could say jobs that are inside and jobs that are outside. Like farmer and sailor are jobs where you work outside."

"A surveyor works mostly outside, too," Rylie said. "My dad is a surveyor," he added proudly.

"OK," I said, "that's one way we can sort the jobs." I drew a horizontal line on the board to serve as a baseline for a bar graph. I placed the farmer, sailor, and surveyor sticky notes one above the other in one column and placed the remaining eight sticky notes one above the other in a second column.

	lawyer
	teacher
	engineer
	mayor
	governor
farmer	congressman
sailor	senator
surveyor	ambassador

"How many more jobs are inside than outside?" I asked. Many hands shot up and I had the children give the answer together in a whisper voice.

"Any other ideas about how we might organize this data?" I asked.

"Maybe works in a city or the country or either," Colin suggested.

"When you say country, do you mean a country like the United States, or do you mean a rural area?" I probed.

"Rural area," Colin answered.

"OK," I said. As I read the occupation on each sticky note, the children told me whether it was a city job, a country job, or if it could be either. I moved the notes into three columns for these three categories. For example, the students decided that an ambassador might travel all around cities and countries but would probably have an office in the city, so they put that job in the *city* category.

The last note I picked up had *sailor* on it. The children were quiet for a moment, and then several commented: "It doesn't fit." "It's none of those." "We need another place."

Colin had a suggestion. "How about a row for *neither?*" he asked.

"Or we could have a separate column for *ocean* or *sea* because a sailor works on a boat," chimed Tosha.

The children agreed that either *ocean* or *neither* would work for sailor. I placed the note with *sailor* on it in a fourth column.

To prepare the students for analyzing their own graphs later, I asked a few questions about the data: "How many more city jobs are there than country jobs?" "How many fewer ocean jobs are there than country jobs?"

city	country	either city or country	ocean or sea
ambassador			
lawyer			
mayor			
congressman		surveyor	
senator		engineer	
governor	farmer	teacher	sailor

Then I asked again, "Any other ideas about how we might organize this data?"

The class was quiet for a moment before Brandon came up with an idea. "I've got it!" he said, excited. "What about *elected* and *not elected?* Can I come up and do it?" I nodded and Brandon came to the board to rearrange the notes. Brandon worked quickly. He placed the first note in the second column somewhat above the line I had drawn, rather than using it as a baseline. This gave me the opportunity to re-inforce the importance of the columns starting at the same baseline.

"That way we can compare the columns and see how many more or fewer are in one than the other," I explained.

Brandon assigned all but the ambassador job to a category. He looked puzzled. I told him that ambassadors are appointed officials and are not elected. He placed the ambassadors at the top of the "Not elected" column, completing the new graph.

elected	not elected
	lawyer
	ambassador
	sailor
mayor	farmer
congressman	surveyor
senator	engineer
governor	teacher

To model an idea that wasn't effective for revealing information about the data, I suggested that we sort the jobs by their beginning letters. The students quickly realized that our graph didn't really tell us anything about the data.

"It's too spread out," Claire frowned.

"It's just a bunch of jobs all by themselves," agreed Nicki.

We discussed how when mathematicians look at data they look at it in a variety of ways because they are not certain which way will reveal the most interesting information. "One reason for classifying data," I told the class, "is to discover what's interesting about it and to help us see what it can tell us. When we organize our data by beginning letter, it doesn't give us any useful information."

I organized the sticky notes back into the previous categories of elected and nonelected. I said, "Now think first by yourself and then share with your neighbor: What you can tell from the data organized this way?" I gave the students time to talk among themselves.

I called them back to attention and said, "Now we're going to gather data about the jobs that *you* might want to have someday. When I was in the second grade, I wanted to be a veterinarian, a dancer, an artist, and a teacher." The students were interested in hearing me share about myself. "In a few minutes, each of you will choose three jobs that you'd like to have when you grow up. Then you'll work in small groups to sort your information in different ways. Finally, you'll decide on one of those ways to represent your data."

Because this was these second graders' first attempt at grouping data in multiple ways, I elected to have them work together in small groups of four. Each group would have twelve pieces of data to sort, which would provide them with enough data to organize without overwhelming them.

I organized the class into groups of four and then gave three unlined 3-by-5-inch index cards to each student. I instructed, "Working quietly by yourself, think of three different jobs you might like to have when you grow up and write one job on each of your three cards."

I gave time for all of the children to record on their cards and then said, "Place your cards in the middle of your group so that you can read one another's career choices and, as a team, talk about ways you can sort your data. Remember that your categories should help us learn more about the jobs you've chosen. Organize your data in at least two different ways before deciding on which way your group wants to share with the class. Then carefully place your cards in columns the way we did together on the board with data from *So You Want to Be President?* When you've done this, stand to show me that you're ready for me to come and discuss with your group." The children had been listening attentively. To give them a little stretch, I said,

"Show me how you'll stand at your table when you're ready for me to come and talk with you."

When the children sat down, I wrapped up the directions. "After I visit your group, you'll take a piece of chart paper," I said, motioning to the paper supply, "paste your data on the paper, label the categories, add a title, and write a few sentences describing what the data show. We'll post our charts for others to view, so make your work clear to others."

As I spoke, I made a list on the board:

Record one occupation on each card.
Organize data in more than one way.
Check with Mrs. P.
Decide on the best way to represent data.
Paste, label, and title graph.
Write statements about graph.

As the students began to work, the room warmed with conversations. I circulated to observe whether the students were flexible in their thinking. Could they organize the data in a variety of ways? Show it in columns? Did they understand that the data could show different things depending on how they organized it?

One group organized their data into three categories—athlete, teacher, and scientist. Eight of the twelve pieces of data fell into the athlete category and the group was having a discussion.

"This way tells us we like sports," David said, making the touchdown signal with his hands.

"But it doesn't tell us anything else, really," Anne added.

"I don't think we should use it," said Bryan.

The four children put their heads together and began to move cards around. When I walked by a few minutes later they seemed stymied.

"Do you see any way of dividing this category into two categories?" I asked pointing to the sports category.

After a few seconds, Courtney's face lit up and she began to move the cards into columns without telling us why. (See page 82.)

"Oh," Anne said, surprised, "Team athletes and individual, like golfer, ice skater, and skier. We hadn't thought about splitting one in two."

"Tell me about these four pieces of data, teacher, teacher, astronaut, and archeologist. Why are they organized like this?" I pressed.

Expecting Courtney to respond because she was the one who had reorganized the cards, I was pleasantly surprised when Bryan spoke up. "Well, teachers, archeologists, and astronauts don't play sports, so they need to be in a different category. And archeologists and

individual sports	team sports	teachers	scientists
	baseball player		
	football player		
skier	football player		
golfer	basketball player	teacher	archeologist
ice skater	hockey player	teacher	astronaut

astronauts are both scientists and teachers are just teachers," Bryan smiled and shrugged.

"Just teachers, huh?" I teased. The group laughed and reassured me that I was the best teacher they knew.

"Now see if you can find a different way of categorizing your data," I said and I left the group chattering. This conversation told me that these students were able to categorize data and decide how the categories did or didn't give them information.

I observed another group of four students discussing which category some of their data fit into. "Should we put fireman with dangerous jobs, or jobs that help people?" inquired Sam.

"Jobs that help people, because they help save houses and buildings from burning," Jasmine reasoned.

"But that's dangerous, because they could get burned or they might have to rescue someone from their house," Maddie countered.

"I think we should put fireman with jobs that help because it fits better with doctor and policeman than with race car driver," Eric stated.

The group seemed to agree with Eric's logic. However, when the children stood, indicating that they were ready for me to visit, I noticed that they no longer had the category for dangerous jobs. (See page 83.)

"Tell me how your group decided on these categories," I inquired.

Maddie began, "Well, we did have five categories—people who help, people who teach, people who entertain, people who work with animals, and people who have dangerous jobs."

"Yeah, but then we only had race car driver in the dangerous category and we decided it also was entertainment, so we moved it," Sam continued.

"We were going to keep the category and add fireman to it so there would be two, but then our graph got too spread out," Eric said.

help	teach	entertain	work with animals
		race car driver	
		basketball player	
fireman		singer	
doctor	teacher	actress	horse trainer
policeman	teacher	comedian	veterinarian

Jasmine noted, "Four categories work better for twelve pieces of information. If we had more pieces, then we could keep people with dangerous jobs."

Students began to post their work around the classroom. The children then circulated around the room looking at one another's graphs and conclusions. They wrote questions and comments on sticky notes and left them for the authors to respond to. I instructed the students that their comments should focus on the organization and content of the graph, not on spelling or neatness. Each group of students then had an opportunity to present its information and respond to any comments or questions it had received.

A Star in My Orange

A Star in My Orange: Looking for Nature's Shapes, by Dana Meachen Rau (2002), is a collection of photos accompanied by a simple text about shapes found in nature. The book begins with the star shape found inside an orange cut crosswise, a tide pool, a snowflake, and a daisy. Next it compares the antlers of a deer and people's own arms and hands to the shapes of tree branches. The book continues introducing hexagons and spirals as they are portrayed in nature. Each two-page spread contains text on one side and a photo on the other. Behind the text are silhouettes of the shape depicted in the corresponding photo.

After reading *A Star in My Orange* to a class of first graders, I used pattern blocks to engage the children in looking at shapes in the world around us.

MATERIALS

chart paper, 1 sheet

pattern blocks, 7 or 8 each of yellow hexagons, red trapezoids, orange squares, and green triangles

4 or 5 oranges

As the class gathered on the floor around me, I handed out oranges for the first graders to examine. Posted behind me was a blank piece of chart paper. Nearby I had a roll of masking tape and a container of pattern blocks that included only yellow hexagons, red trapezoids, orange squares, and green triangles. I had removed the tan and blue parallelograms because narrowing our study was necessary to the success of the lesson at this point in the year. I planned to conduct a similar activity later in the year using both the tan and blue parallelograms.

I began by asking the students to tell me the shape of the oranges they were holding.

"It's a ball shape," said Ally.

"A circle," offered Camila.

"It's round," Jeffrey shared.

"What sort of shapes do you think we might find on the inside of an orange if we cut it in half?" I asked. I took a permanent marker and drew around the orange I was holding to show how I would cut it crosswise. There were many ohs and ahhs as I marked on the fruit. A couple of students responded that they thought a circle would be found inside, while a few thought that they would see a triangle.

I showed the class the book and said, "*A Star in My Orange* is a book about looking at nature's shapes."

The students became excited. "I see it! I see it! I see the star!" several exclaimed as they pointed to the photo of the orange on the cover.

After reading the book through once to the class, I went back and again showed the children the spreads that show hexagons in nature. I read, "I see lots of little shapes in a turtle's shell, and a bee's honeycomb, and a fallen pinecone." I directed the children to look behind the words at the silhouettes of the hexagons, telling them, "These shapes are called hexagons." I had the children count aloud the sides of several of the silhouetted hexagons to show that each hexagon had six sides.

"We have some tubs of materials for our classroom that have hexagons in them," I said. Reaching into the container of pattern blocks by my side, I held up a yellow hexagon and together we counted its sides. Next I titled the posted chart paper *Pattern Blocks* and underneath wrote *hexagon*. I placed a rolled piece of masking tape on one side of the hexagon pattern block and stuck it on the chart paper next to the word.

Next I said to the children, "There are some other shapes in this container, too." I pulled a green triangle pattern block from the container and held it up for the children to see. Most knew the name and called it out right away. I wrote *triangle* on the chart, rolled another small piece of masking tape, and stuck the pattern block next to the word.

I repeated this with the orange square, which the students could recognize by both name and shape. I added the word *square* to the chart and taped a square pattern block next to it. The students then described a square shape and named many things in their world that were square.

Janey began: "It has four sides. And it looks like a box. A little box."

Benjamin said, "A square has four corners like this window—it has four corners."

Our window is rectangular, but I let Benjamin's example stand and simply said, "The window does have four corners. It is called a *rectangle*. A square is a very special type of rectangle because all of its sides are equal length."

Trevor's hand remained high. "The rug that we sit on is square and it has lots of squares on it."

Trevor's description was correct. The first graders sit on a square rug that has five rows of five color squares each. The squares help define where the children sit.

The last shape I introduced to the class was the trapezoid. I pulled a red trapezoid pattern block from the container along with another hexagon. I placed the trapezoid over the hexagon so that the children could see the relationship between the two shapes.

"It's like the yellow one," Dena said, referring to the hexagon pattern block.

"Yeah, but it's only half," Peter added.

"Yes, it's one-half of a hexagon," I said. "This shape is called a *trapezoid*." I wrote *trapezoid* on the chart and taped a trapezoid pattern block next to it.

Then I reviewed the chart with the children, reading the names of the shapes as I pointed to each.

Pattern Blocks

hexagon

triangle

square

trapezoid

I explained what we were going to do next: "You'll each choose a pattern block from the container. Then we'll go for a walk together.

Your job is to see if you can find any examples of your shape as we walk. You may have to look very closely, so we will walk very slowly and be shape detectives." The students were clearly excited about our activity. Each of them quickly selected a favorite shape. Before we left the classroom, I had each child identify which shape he or she had chosen.

Because it was chilly outside, our walk was through the hallways of our school, which led us through the cafeteria and the media center. At first the students were uncertain about where to look. I prompted them by saying, "I notice Katie is looking up high and low for her triangle shape." As students do, many of them began to look up and down the hall, inspecting every inch of the space.

Malcolm was the first of many who found his shape. "A square," he declared, pointing at the square glass display case. The display case held instruments from around the world, which gave us several more examples of triangles, trapezoids, and hexagons.

Our walk through the cafeteria brought many discoveries. The students found triangles in the pendant flags that hung from the ceiling and squares in the tables, floor tiles, and decorative wall tiles. Lunch was not being served at this time, so I asked the cooks if I could show the students a lunch tray. On it they were able to identify four more squares and a rectangle, the shapes that form the sections of the tray. The children spied a hexagon in the cutout in the back of each chair.

The trapezoid was most elusive. Seth was convinced that he had found a trapezoid in the negative space formed between the drinking fountain spout and basin. It was close, but we found a better example with a telephone's receiver and base. The place where the receiver comes to rest on the base creates a trapezoid shape.

When we returned to the classroom, some of the students still had not discovered a shape independently, and they were determined to do so. I organized the children who had found shapes into four groups, one for each shape. "Talk together about the examples of your shape that you saw on the walk," I instructed. While those students shared in small groups, the few students who had not yet discovered their shape continued their walk around our classroom and were very successful.

To wrap up the lesson, I gave each child a piece of white paper. Each drew a picture of his or her shape and where it had been seen, then taped their pattern block to the illustration.

I posted the "Pattern Block" chart near where the materials are housed in the classroom. After the students shared their papers with the class, I hung them around the room and in the hallway. (See Figures 14–1, 14–2, and 14–3.)

Figure 14–1: Both Alexandra and Carson found triangles in our classroom, one in the middle of the capital letter A and the other hidden in the neck of the overhead projector.

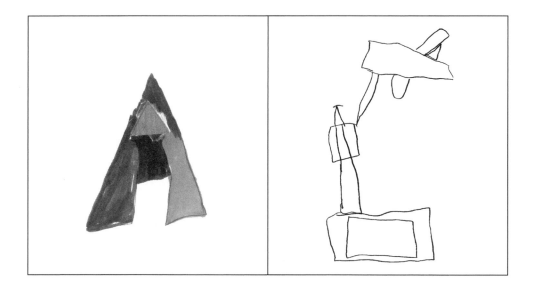

Figure 14–2: After much searching, Mick found a hexagon shape in the cutout of a classroom chair.

Figure 14–3: Lewis and Tania discovered trapezoids in the stem of a pumpkin and the space between a telephone's receiver and its base.

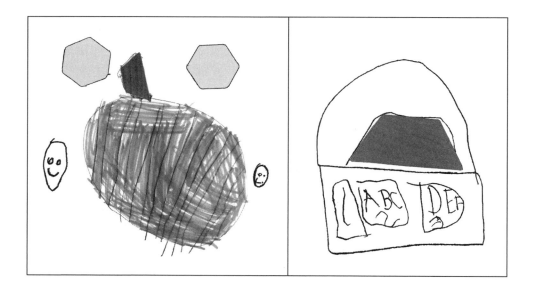

Telling Time

Telling Time: How to Tell Time on Digital and Analog Clocks! by Jules Older (2001) is a comprehensive look at why and how we tell time. The book begins with one question, "What is time?" then explains that time is *when* things happen and *how long* things take. It introduces ways of measuring time, beginning with clock increments of seconds, minutes, and hours and continuing with calendar increments of days, weeks, months, years, decades, centuries, and millennia. The remainder the book emphasizes telling time on both analog and digital clocks.

In the first of the two lessons taught here, first graders learn about what time is in very fundamental ways. Using their daily classroom schedule, they study time in terms of "when things happen." They extend their study to "how long things take," studying such smaller chunks of time as seconds, minutes, and hours. In the second lesson, which extends over several days, second graders learn how to tell time to the nearest minute using both analog and digital clocks.

MATERIALS

First-Grade Lesson

your daily classroom schedule, posted on chart paper

3-by-5-inch unruled note cards, 8–12

digital timer to display on the overhead projector

stopwatch or analog wall clock

Second-Grade Lesson

analog wall clock

battery-powered digital clocks, 1 per group of students

***What Time Is It?* worksheet,** 1 per student initially, then more as needed (see Blackline Masters)

A Lesson with First Grades

It was early in the year when I used the book *Telling Time* with a first-grade class. I wanted the students to think about time in the context of when things would happen in our day at school. I also wanted them to grapple with the concept of how long things take, using basic measurements of seconds, minutes, and hours.

When the students came to the rug that day, our daily schedule hung on the board in front of them. Although it was a routine they had been following for several weeks, I had not marked each of the activities slated on our schedule with a time.

"Today I have a book that is going to help us better understand our daily schedule and teach us about when things happen and how long things take. I'm going to read just the first few pages of the book today. We can finish the book on another day if you like, but today we only need the first part of the book for our lesson."

I read the first seven pages of the book, which includes information about what time is—when things happen, how long things take, and why we tell time—and discusses small chunks of time—second, minute, and hour. I stopped reading before the author introduces the calendar. The students had plenty of information to think about from just the first few pages.

To share the book, I read the main text on each page and then read the content in the conversation bubbles, which clarify the concept being presented. "Time is: When things happen. And time is: How long things take," I read and then proceeded reading the four captions that accompany the illustrations on the page. The four pictures show young children doing various tasks throughout a typical day.

On the next page, "How Long Things Take," there are five scenarios each with its own text box telling how long the activity pictured takes. The illustration the students enjoyed most was labeled "It takes two hours to clean up my room." Some of them could identify with the child who was portrayed finding a sock, a partly eaten sandwich, and many other odds and ends under the bed. Others said their rooms were very tidy and would only take five to ten minutes to clean up. A few students said it would take them no time at all because their room was always clean.

I continued reading about why we tell time and about telling time in little chunks using clocks or watches. I stopped and asked the students to think about our daily schedule and when things happen. "We've been in school for a few weeks now and this is the daily schedule that we follow on most days. This is the order in which things happen for us here at school. I was hoping that you could help me today by adding some times to our schedule. Let's take a look at the first thing posted: Arrival. Does anyone know what time you arrive at school? What time does school begin?"

Most of the students answered, "Eight-thirty." I wrote *Arrival* on the board. Next to it I wrote the time in words—*eight-thirty*—and numerically—*8:30*. (You could write the times directly on your posted existing schedule if you prefer.)

We addressed many, but not all, of the parts of our day listed on the schedule, identifying times for snack time; special events such as art, music, physical education, and technology; lunch; recess; and dismissal. These parts of the day never changed; the times for academic activities in the day, such as math, science, and literacy lessons, blend together.

"So time means *when* things happen," I said. "These times show when things happen in our school day. Now I want you to think about the way that time helps us know *how long* things take." I opened the book to the first full spread and pointed to a picture of a boy brushing his teeth. I read the caption, "It takes two minutes to brush my teeth." Then I said, "I hope that all of you brushed your teeth this morning before school. How long do you think it took you to brush your teeth?"

"About five minutes," Brendan thought.

"One whole minute, because I counted to a hundred in my head. That is what my mom told me to do," Gabriella shared.

"My dentist said to hum the ABC song in my head three times when I brush my teeth, and I didn't have any cavities when I went to the dentist last time," Sophia said.

"I think it was pretty long, like three minutes," Matt said, thrusting three fingers into the air.

"I'd like you to predict how much time some tasks in our classroom take," I said. "Then we'll time how long they actually take. I'll choose tasks that many of you do daily. I think this will help you better understand just how long it should take you to complete those tasks." The children seemed interested in hearing what came next.

I said, "Let's start with our routine when we arrive, like unpacking your backpack, taking off your jacket, and putting your lunch in the tub if you brought one from home. A few students will act this out while the rest of us will time them." I pulled down the screen and turned on the overhead projector to show the digital timer I had placed on it. (If you don't have a digital timer available, you could use a stop watch or an analog wall clock with a second hand.)

"Randal, Hillary, Hayden, and Charise, would you help demonstrate for us?" I asked. They nodded and got up. I instructed them to put their jackets on, grab their backpacks from their lockers, then pretend that they were just entering the classroom for the day. The four of them went outside and then entered the room, took off their jackets and hung them on hooks inside their lockers, then pretended to unpack and hang up their backpacks. Finally they came back to the rug.

As the four children demonstrated how long "Arrival" took, the rest of us watched the seconds go by on the screen. When all four of them had come to the rug, I stopped the timer. It read 1:54.

"One minute and fifty-four seconds," I read. "This is almost two minutes, and I bet if we had on our winter gear like hats, mittens, boots, and heavy coats, it would take more time, maybe five minutes. And if more kids were over in the locker area at once, it might take even longer, like ten minutes." I recorded on a 3-by-5-inch note card and posted it above the lockers.

Arrival

5–10 minutes

five to ten minutes

"Many of you use the pencil sharpener during the day. About how long do you think it takes to sharpen your pencil?"

"Maybe a minute," guessed Xavier.

"Less than a minute," said Erica.

"Five minutes?" offered Daniel uncertainly.

"Let's find out how much time it takes to sharpen your pencil," I said.

We acted this out as we had with the first scenario. Four students happily obliged, sharpening their pencils one at a time. For each child, I recorded on the overhead timer how long it took to walk from the table to the sharpener, sharpen the pencil, and return to the table.

We collected four times: 43 seconds, 1 minute and 11 seconds, 1 minute and 2 seconds, 58 seconds. Because the recorded times were out of the realm of what I would expect first graders to understand, I read the times and stated how they compared to one minute. "Forty-three seconds is *less* than a minute. One minute and eleven seconds is *more* than a minute. One minute and two seconds is *about* a minute. Fifty-eight seconds is *almost* a minute."

Finally I summarized, "So each of you took about a minute to complete the task of walking to the pencil sharpener, sharpening your pencil, and returning to your seat." I wrote: *pencil sharpening 1 minute—one minute* on a note card and asked a student to post the card above the pencil sharpener mounted on the wall.

We continued our lesson in a similar manner, timing a variety of tasks. I selected both tasks that were fun—dancing to our theme song, "We Are Family"; singing the alphabet song—and tasks that typically come up during the school day—getting a drink, washing hands, lining up to leave the classroom.

This was a fun way to practice daily procedures while adding the concept of how long things take. Posting the times proved useful later: Because the students had observed about how much time each task should take and the note cards were posted to remind them, they seemed to become more cognizant of how they used and managed time.

A Lesson with Second Graders

With the second graders gathered around, I read *Telling Time*. The children seemed very interested in the book and eager about learning to tell time.

"I know that many of you already know a lot about the clock that hangs on our wall. What are some things you can tell me about it?"

Trevor began: "It has numbers on it."

"Which numbers?" I questioned.

"One, two, three, four, five, six, seven, eight, nine, ten, eleven, and twelve," he rattled off, with some of his peers joining in.

"What else can you tell me about the clock on the wall?"

"There are lots of little lines on it," Caroline said.

"I know what the lines are for," Leif volunteered. "They show the minutes, like five, ten, fifteen."

"There are hands on the clock that go around and point to the time," Annika added.

Getting back to the lines on the clock face, Andrea said, "I think there are sixty lines on the clock, because there are sixty minutes in an hour."

After other students had contributed to our discussion, I opened the book to the spread where both analog and digital clocks are introduced. I read from the page to summarize what we had just discussed: "An analog clock has little numbers around the edge and hands that point to the numbers." I added, "The clock on our classroom wall is an analog clock."

I read, "A digital clock has big numbers in the middle. Here's a digital clock." I put the book down beside me and showed the children one of the battery-operated digital clocks I had brought to class for the lesson and set to reflect the same time as our analog wall clock.

We discussed the similarities of the two types of clocks—both have numbers; use seconds, minutes, and hours; and tell what time it is. Then I explained the lesson: "Today each group will get a digital clock on their table. We are going to study both the analog clock on the wall and the digital clock on the table, to help us learn to tell time."

I asked the students to go back to the rectangular tables where they sit, six to a table. For this lesson, I asked children who sat at the ends of tables to move their chairs to one of the longer sides, so that everyone could see the digital clocks. As the students moved, I placed a battery-operated digital clock on each table and distributed copies of the *What Time Is It?* worksheet.

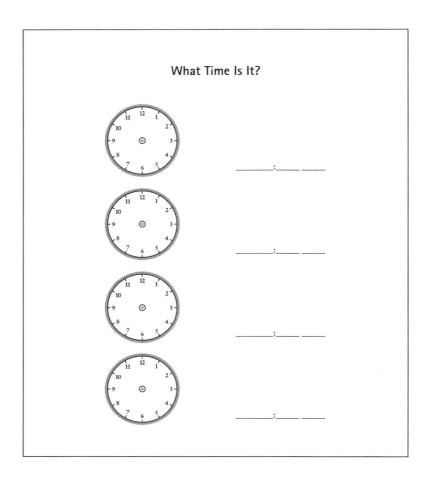

I explained that we would be recording the time shown on the analog clock on our wall and the corresponding time on the digital clock. I asked if anyone had any questions. A few students claimed that they could not see the wall clock very well from their seats, so we moved them to other places in the room. Before beginning I reminded the students to use pencil and to pay attention to only the black hour and minute hands on our analog wall clock. "I'm not interested now in the red second hand," I told them.

To begin, I asked the class to look at the digital clocks on their tables and record exactly what they saw in the first digital clock blanks on their papers. The students recorded *1:50*. I said, "Now study the analog clock on the wall and record the matching time on your paper, directly beside the digital time you just recorded."

The classroom was hushed as the students concentrated on studying the clock on the wall and recording its precise time. Some of the children busily erased, trying to get the hands just right. Others squinted at the clock, back at their papers, then at the clock again to confirm what they had decided about where to draw the hands.

We did this over the next twenty minutes, noting the times 1:50, 1:55, 2:00, and 2:03. I deliberately started with times where the minute hand is on the five-minute marks, then threw in the last time to see what the students would do with it. When the students had recorded the last time on their papers, some asked if we could do this again.

"Yes," I responded. "Tomorrow we'll practice more."

"Can we keep the clocks on our tables?" Aaron asked, voicing many of the students' thoughts.

"Sure," I replied. There were cheers throughout the classroom. Because the digital clocks ran on batteries and didn't pose a safety issue, I had planned to leave them on the desks. The clocks created high interest and spontaneity throughout the remainder of the school day. The students timed themselves doing other tasks, like writing their names on their papers, writing a letter to their parents in the Family Journal, using the bathroom, getting a drink, and so on. They were mesmerized by the clocks and responded positively when I said to them, "We have just five minutes to straighten up the room and put away our supplies to get ready to go home."

After the students left for the day, I looked through their work to see where the following day's lesson needed to begin. I wasn't sure if they would need more of the same or some reteaching, or if we could move on to telling time to the nearest minute rather than to the nearest five minutes.

Based on what I had seen in the students' papers, the next day I reviewed the purposes of the big and little hands on the analog clock, rereading the pages in the book *Telling Time* that address this. I read, "Now let's look at analog clocks, the ones with hands. . . . Clocks have three kinds of hands: little hands, big hands, and second hands. . . . Big hands tell the minutes. Little hands tell the hours. Second hands tell the seconds. So how do you tell time with hands?" I turned the page and continued reading, engaging the students with the book's further explanations of clock hands.

We repeated the recording activity of the day before, but this time I asked the students to record a time from the analog wall clock first, then note the corresponding time on the digital clock. I could see that the students benefited from this additional practice.

The following day I returned to the activity, mixing in more times that weren't on five-minute increments. In general, the students did very well, accurately reading and recording the time to the nearest minute.

After several days of revisiting the book and practicing with both the digital and analog clocks visible, I covered the faces of the digital clocks on the students' tables, using a note card attached with a single piece of masking tape at the top so that the students could flip the card up and check the time. I used note cards because they are sturdier than paper and because the students couldn't see through them.

The students were visibly excited about the new challenge. I conducted the lesson in much the same way as before, having the children look at the analog wall clock and record the time by drawing in minute and hour hands. This time the students recorded what the digital clock should read without looking at the digital faces. They loved flipping up the note cards to check if they were correct. A few times the digital clocks had already changed to the next minute by the time the students flipped the cards up. I suggested that children who worked at a slower rate keep up with the class by simply recording the digital clock readings on their papers and then they could go back and record what the analog "match" would be for that particular time. This minor adjustment worked for all but two students. These two needed a simplified assignment, so I had them work on completing just two of the four clocks on the worksheet.

The next day, I covered the wall clock with a 9-by-12-inch piece of black construction paper. The students' enthusiasm was evident as they anticipated what they would be practicing that day. During this session, the students first recorded the time displayed on the digital clocks on their tables. Then I prompted them to draw hands on the analog clocks on their papers to show the same time. After this I flipped up the black construction paper to reveal the analog clock face. Most of the children celebrated with a "Yes!" cheer, expressing it silently as I've taught them to do. Others busily erased, perfecting their work or making changes.

Throughout this series of lessons, every student made gains in learning about time and how we measure it. All students learned how to distinguish between the minute hand and the hour hand on our analog wall clock. All learned to interpret what the time those hands represent would look like when displayed on a digital clock. All learned what an analog and a digital clock were and could explain the difference. All learned how to read a digital clock correctly. All learned to tell time to the nearest five minutes on an analog clock. Most students were able to tell time to the nearest minute on an analog clock. Most, when given a time expressed digitally, were able to record the corresponding time on an analog clock, and vice versa.

The use of real clocks and the informative book *Telling Time* contributed to the successful learning in our classroom. The students were actively involved in learning about measuring time. Their interest in the digital clocks was so high that I decided to keep one digital clock in our room for the remainder of the year. I placed the digital clock on the opposite side of the room from the analog wall clock. Randomly throughout the year, I would ask students what time it was. This gave me an opportunity to see which clock they referred to. Some would look to the analog clock while others checked the digital clock. For those who relied heavily on the digital clock, I would ask, "Can you tell me what time the analog clock reads?" These informal assessments gave me information about which students would benefit from additional lessons and practice.

What Is Square?

Rebecca Kai Dotlich's *What Is Square?* (1999) contains colorful photos of objects that are familiar in a child's world, accompanied by simple rhyming text.

In this lesson, kindergartners look for squares in the everyday objects shown in the book, then look for squares in the classroom. The young students become familiar with the shape and with the attributes that make something square. The extension lesson, a sorting activity, helps further children's geometric understanding as they differentiate between squares and other shapes.

MATERIALS

1 large clear tub

1 large grocery bag

Triscuit, Wheat Thins, and graham crackers, 1 box of each

1 strip of white paper, about 3-by-9 inches, labeled *What Is Square?*

a variety of round, square, and triangular objects

sorting mats, enough to support a learning center

With the students seated on the rug in front of me, I began by displaying the cover of the book *What Is Square?* and reading the title aloud. I then opened the book and read, "A biscuit, a basket, a patch on your knee," pointing to the photograph of each square object as I mentioned it. The children were immediately drawn into the book. Many inspected their own jeans to see if a square patch like the one pictured in the book was needed or would fit. The story continued to captivate the students with its scrumptious pictures of caramels, crackers, waffles, and brownies. The children marveled at a close-up photo of a checkerboard, commenting that the game board itself made a square and that the many black and red spaces covering the checkerboard were also squares. The rhymes in the text, which name what is square on each page, played a role in holding the students' interest.

The book's last spread shows items that the earlier pages don't. Most of them are square, but others are round, triangular, star-shaped, and circular. The text asks, "What else is SQUARE? Your turn to look!" The students were eager to name the items. I called on volunteers to come up one at a time and point to a square object. This allowed me to see which students were able to distinguish square items from various other shapes.

(The book concludes with, "A mirror, a map, a brownie, a book." The book pictured *What Is Round?*, another in author Dotlich's shapes series. Both titles are out of print, but I later found *What Is Round?* and *What Is Triangle?* in our school's media center and the public library and conducted similar lessons to this one.)

We read the book again, with the students sharing in the reading of the rhyming text. This time I ended with my own question: "What is special about things that are square?"

"Squares all have four sides," Ryan said.

"What about those sides? Are they all the same length?" I asked.

The students weren't quite sure about this; some nodded their heads "yes." Others shook their heads "no" and looked unsure. I took boxes of Triscuits, Wheat Thins, and graham crackers from the grocery bag I had close by. I wanted the students to differentiate between squares and rectangles, and to learn that squares are a special kind of rectangle that has all four sides equal.

"All of these crackers are rectangles, but only two of them are special rectangles called squares. Which ones do you think are the squares?" I asked the class.

The students easily answered correctly, naming or pointing to the boxes of Triscuit and Wheat Thins. "Ryan said earlier that squares have four sides. He's right. These graham crackers have four sides, too, but they're not square like the Triscuit and Wheat Thins. What is special about the four sides of a square?" I asked. "Miriam?"

"They are the same," she said.

"What does Miriam mean by 'they are the same'?" I asked the group.

"The sides are the same size," Nathaniel stated.

"The sides are the same, not long and short like the graham crackers," Isabelle tried to clarify.

Because the kindergartners' vocabularies were limited, I stated their idea in several other ways: "You are very observant. A square's sides are all the same. All four sides are the same length. Each one is as long as the others. A square's sides are equal in length." As I spoke, I traced the sides of a square Triscuit and then of a square Wheat Thins.

"What else can you say about squares?" I asked.

Sasha said, "They have four points."

"What do you mean by 'four points'?" I asked.

Sasha did not have the vocabulary to describe them as "four corners," so she came up and counted, "one, two, three, four," touching each corner of the square on the front cover of the book.

"Sasha is right, there are four corners or points on a square. What else can you tell me about things that are square?"

"They can be big or small," shared Miranda.

"They can have lots of squares in them," Thomas said.

To help Thomas make his point, I turned to the page featuring the square dishcloth, window, and waffle. "Yeah, like that," Thomas said. "The waffle has lots of little squares in it."

"The towel has lots of little squares, too," Caspar jumped in.

"And so does the window," added Jacinto. "It has one, two, three, four squares in it."

I expanded our discussion of the differences between a square and a rectangle to our classroom windows, which are rectangular but have some square panes. "What about the windows in our classroom?" I asked. "Can you see the little squares in the windows?" The children shifted their attention to the windows.

I decided to have the kindergartners use movement to strengthen their learning. I asked them to stand and said, "With your feet still and a pretend pencil in your hand, carefully draw a square. Watch me do it first." I modeled drawing a large square in the air, counting as I did so: "One, two, three, four sides." The students did the same, counting the sides as they drew in the air.

"Let's do it again and count the corners," I said. We did this together.

"Let's do it again and remember to make the sides equal in length so we're drawing squares, not rectangles," I said, adding, "Today we're learning about special rectangles that are squares." This activity supported kinesthetic learning and released some kindergartner energy. We continued, with the children drawing squares slowly and then more quickly, counting the sides or corners each time. To wind them down, we used our fingers to draw little squares in the air, just like the ones in the dishtowel, the waffle, and our window.

I had the children sit down again and I explained the next activity. I showed them a large clear tub into which I had placed the boxes of Triscuit and Wheat Thins. "Today we're going to search for things in our classroom that are square and place them in this giant tub. Remember that squares have four sides and four corners, and all the sides are the same length."

I had written *What Is Square?* on a strip of white paper. I attached this label to the tub with masking tape. I told the students that I would play our quiet music (music we play during quiet times of the day) for five minutes. During that time they should walk quietly around the classroom searching for just one item they could place into our "What Is Square?" tub. I explained that the square thing should be small enough to carry. If it was too big or couldn't be moved, like our square windowpanes, I would provide paper for them to draw a picture of the item.

"If you finish before I stop the music," I said, "come back and sit in your square on our rectangle rug." The students began to notice that the rug they sit on each day was made up of rows of squares that formed a rectangle.

I started the music and the search began. I hadn't explained that the corners of squares have to be ninety degrees, as this is beyond the understanding of typical kindergartners. But it wasn't an issue for them; all of the examples they found were truly square. The students clearly enjoyed searching the classroom for square objects. Some of them moved slowly as if to sneak up on items. Others stood in the middle of the room and slowly rotated, taking in the entire room before heading off in the direction where they had spotted a square object.

As the five minutes ended, I had to encourage a few students to join the rest of us on the rug. It wasn't that they couldn't find a square, but rather that they couldn't decide which square item to bring. One student needed extra time to draw a picture of the object she found, the art table, because it was too big to carry.

Once the children were seated, I had each in turn come up to the front, share their square item, and place it in the "What Is Square?" tub. Several students brought square books, but Omar brought one that was clearly more rectangular in shape. As he showed his item to his peers, several hands went up.

"I don't think that's a square," Ally said. "I think that's a rectangle."

Omar looked at the book with a critical eye and shrugged. I helped him by asking, "What do you think, Omar—if you trace the sides of the book with your finger, do two of the sides feel longer than the others?" He did this and nodded "yes." "Do you think you can find a book that has all four sides equal?" Omar nodded again and seemed comfortable, but I let him choose a helper to go with him to the book area and help find a square-shaped book.

Jessica brought a lunch box, which was rectangular in shape. I handled this in a similar manner. She and a partner searched the tub where we store lunches and found no square-shaped lunch boxes, so they had to find a completely different item.

The items that the children found included a pad of 3-by-3-inch sticky notes, a computer disc, a CD case, dice, and various math manipulatives including Unifix cubes, square color tiles, and a square puzzle piece. Kylie and Warren contributed the containers we use to hold art supplies. Although the sides of the containers are rectangular, both students pointed out to their classmates that the tops of the containers are square.

Extension

I placed a tub of mixed objects, some round, some square, and some triangular, at a learning center and added a sorting mat to place objects on. The students were to sort the shapes into two distinct categories—square and not square.

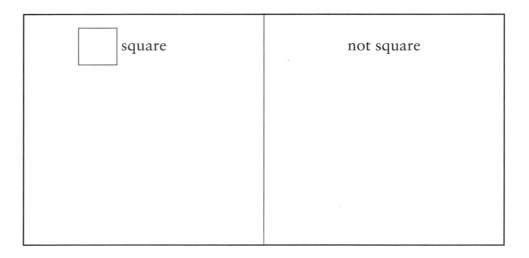

The *What Is Square?* activity was a fun way for the children to learn about shapes. It was meaningful because the objects were relevant to the students' world. The children learned the different attributes of a square through collecting, handling, and sorting objects, and they learned vocabulary that they used when talking about the square objects with their peers.

As we walked through the hallways and media center of our school, the students continually made connections, finding square objects in the world around them. As we filed into the cafeteria later that week, Ghada said, "There are squares on our plates," about the cafeteria trays with the compartments for various food items.

Through this explicit exploration of the shapes in our everyday world, the five- and six-year-olds began to see how shapes—in this case, squares—were all around them.

What's a Pair?
What's a Dozen?

Using bright photographs of children in everyday situations, Stephen Swinburne's *What's a Pair? What's a Dozen?* (2000) presents cardinal and ordinal numbers and introduces vocabulary associated with numbers, including *single, pair, double, couple, triple, several, few,* and *many.* The book also introduces the prefixes *uni-, bi-,* and *tri-* and provides photo riddles to help enforce children's understanding of the terminology in the book.

The lesson taught here helps first graders sort words and numbers into those that tell position and those that tell how many and think about examples for both categories.

MATERIALS

chart paper, 2 pieces

3-by-5-inch index cards, 3, labeled *first, second,* and *third*

items that illustrate *pairs, doubles, several, few, many,* **and** *a dozen,* placed in a bag

To prepare, I labeled three 3-by-5-inch index cards *first, second,* and *third* and posted on the board two pieces of 12-by-18-inch drawing paper to use as charts in the lesson. I placed items in a bag to illustrate pairs, doubles, few, many, and a dozen—a pair of socks, a set of double-print photographs, four plastic cups in a stack, a box of eight crayons, a box of sixty-four crayons, and an empty egg carton. I had the bag nearby when I gathered the first graders to read the book *What's a Pair? What's a Dozen?*

"Everything starts with one," I read, showing the class the four beautiful photographs on the page. I asked, "What things on the page show the number one?"

"A dog, and he looks just like my grandpa's dog," Kendal said, referring to the photograph of a dog lying on hay in front of a barn door. "And he lives on a farm, too."

"A balloon. It's a hot air balloon," Tara said.

"A rooster, and he's running in the grass," Stephen said.

"What else on the page shows the number one?" I asked.

"The moon," several children chorused, referring to the magnificent photo of a full moon rising over a cityscape.

Each of the next two pages in the book introduces a word that relates to one—*single* and *first*—defining it with a sentence that relates to the photograph. I read, "A single ball is one ball." Veronica commented about the photograph, which shows a girl playing with a large blue ball: "There's one girl, too." The next page shows a group of children lined up, with the first child raising her hand. I read, "If you are first in line, you are before all others." The following page introduces the prefix *uni* and illustrates it with a photograph of a girl riding a unicycle.

The book explains that "When you have two of something, you have a pair" to introduce the number two. The children easily identified the pair in each of the four photos on the page—horses, shoes, telephone booths, and children. The following pages illustrate more words that relate to two—*couple, second,* and *double.* The prefix *bi* is introduced with a photograph of a boy riding a bicycle.

The book then introduces the number three, presenting related words—*triple* and *third*—and the prefix *tri.* It continues with other vocabulary that relates to numbers—*several, few, many, odd, even, half dozen, dozen,* and *baker's dozen.* (*Several* is defined in the book as "more than two or three," *few* as "a small number," and *many* as "a large number.") The students enjoyed hearing the book and seeing children who looked much like themselves in the photographs. They also enjoyed the photos at the end of the book and the questions asked for each—for example, "Can you find the pair?" "Which one is the unicycle?" "Who's first in line?"

After finishing reading the book, I introduced the lesson. "This book has many words in it that mean one, two, three, and more," I began. "Some of the words refer to the position or order of things, and some of the words refer to amounts and tell us how many there are." I titled the two pieces of paper I had posted on the board "Position" and "How Many."

"Do you remember the pages in the book where the children were in line?" I asked. The children nodded their heads. I turned to the first page that showed this and reread, "If you are first in line, you are before all others." Then I explained, "The word *first* here refers to the girl's position in the line."

I turned to another page and read, "Second and double are other words for two. If you are second in line, you come after the first person." I asked Hunter, Veronica, and Bruce to come up and help me demonstrate this idea by standing in a line and facing the windows.

"Which position in line is Hunter in?" I asked.

"First," bellowed the students. I handed Hunter the 3-by-5-inch card with "first" on it and asked him to hold it so that the children seated could see it.

I then asked, "Which position in line is Veronica in?" The class responded with ease: "Second." I handed Veronica the card with "second" on it and asked her to hold is so that the others could see it. I repeated this for Bruce, handing him the card with "third" on it.

I asked the three students in line to turn and face the opposite direction. This put Bruce first in line, Veronica second, and Hunter third. I asked them to hold their cards up high so we could see them. "Now are they still in the same position?" I asked.

"No," answered all the children except Aaron. He explained his idea: "Well, you asked us if they were in the same position. Well, Veronica *is* in the same position, but Bruce and Hunter are in different positions." Not all of the children followed Aaron's reasoning, but I knew that it would be clarified when I asked the children in line to change cards to show their new positions.

"Which card should Bruce have now?" I asked.

Michael replied, "Now Bruce is first, not third, and Hunter is third, not first."

"Yeah, they should trade cards," Elizabeth added. The rest agreed and the two boys swapped cards.

"What about Veronica? Does she need a different card?" I asked.

"No," the children responded.

"She's still in the middle," Tara said.

"So Veronica is still in the second position," I said to reinforce the use of the correct terminology.

I turned to the two charts I had labeled and said, "*First, second,* and *third* are words we use to tell what position things are in. In this instance, we used them to tell about the order of the children, which place each had in line." Next to the title "Position" on the first chart, I wrote *order* and *place in line*. Below I listed the ordinal numbers as words and also, in parentheses, numerically:

first (1st)
second (2d)
third (3d)

Still referring to the three children in line at the front of the classroom, I asked, "How many children are in line?"

"Three," the students answered.

"And how many boys are in line?" I continued.

"Two," they responded.

"And how many girls are in line?" I asked.

"One," they said.

"Now turn the other way again," I instructed Bruce, Hunter, and Veronica. Bruce and Hunter quickly exchanged cards. I repeated the three questions I'd asked before: "How many children are in line?" "How many boys are in line?" "How many girls are in line?"

I said to the class, "When I asked you how many, your answers stayed the same no matter which way the children were facing and no matter which position each was in. That's because the words *one, two,* and *three* don't tell us anything about the order of the children or their position in line. They tell us how many children there are." On the chart titled "How Many," I listed the words and wrote the numeral in parentheses after each:

one (1)
two (2)
three (3)

I continued this list, writing words and numerals for the numbers up to twelve:

one (1)	*seven (7)*
two (2)	*eight (8)*
three (3)	*nine (9)*
four (4)	*ten (10)*
five (5)	*eleven (11)*
six (6)	*twelve (12)*

I revisited other words introduced in the book—*single, pair, couple, double, triple, several, few, many, dozen, half dozen,* and *baker's dozen*—asking for each whether I should write it on the Position chart or the How Many chart. I didn't include *odd* and *even* because they don't refer to either cardinal or ordinal numbers, but rather to a way to classify cardinal numbers. To revisit the words, I referred to the book and used the bag of items I had collected. First I pulled out a pair of socks from the bag.

"How many socks are there?" I asked.

"Two," the children chorused.

"So two belongs on our how many chart," I said.

"It's already there," Aaron pointed out.

"What's another word that we use when we talk about two matching socks?" I asked.

"Pair," the children answered with ease.

"So pair also tells us how many there are, that there are two of something," I said, and wrote *pair* on the chart next to *two (2)*.

I pulled the set of double prints out of the bag. "When I took my film to be developed, I asked for double prints," I said. "This is what I got. How many of each photograph are there?"

"Two," they answered.

"So double can also tell us that there are two of something," I said, and wrote *double* on the chart next to *pair*.

"There are many other words introduced in the book, too," I said. I flipped through the book to find the photograph of a child eating a triple-dip ice cream cone. We talked about the picture and I added *triple* to the How Many chart next to *three (3)*.

Showing the children the book's cover, I said, "In fact, the title, *What's a Pair? What's a Dozen?* contains one of the words." I took the empty egg carton from my bag. "How many are a dozen eggs?"

"Twelve," responded the class. We counted the spaces for the eggs by ones and then checked by counting by twos.

"So *dozen* refers to *how many* and tells us that there are twelve of something." I wrote *dozen* on the How Many chart after *twelve (12)*.

"Sometimes words refer to *how many* but don't tell us a specific amount," I said. I turned to the spread in the book that introduces *few* and *many*. I read, "Some gardens have only a small number of flowers. They have few flowers. Some gardens have a large number of flowers. They have many flowers." I pointed to the photograph on the left and asked, "How many flowers does the word *few* refer to in this picture?" The students studied the picture and decided just two.

I took two boxes of crayons out of the bag, one with eight crayons and the other with sixty-four. I held the boxes up so that the children could see them. I asked, "How many crayons does the word *few* mean when I'm talking about the small box of crayons?"

"Eight," answered the class.

We discussed the idea that the word *few* tells *how many*, but can mean different numbers, as we had just seen with two and eight. I said, "Sometimes *a few* depends on what we're talking about. If I said, take a few apples, you might take just two or three. But if I said, take a few peanuts, you might take a small handful of six or ten or more." I turned to the How Many chart and wrote *few* to the right of the numbers, but not next to any particular one. Beneath it I wrote *many*.

How Many?

	One (1)	
Pair, Double	*Two (2)*	
Triple	*Three (3)*	
	Four (4)	*Few*
	Five (5)	*Many*
	Six (6)	*Several*
	Seven (7)	
	Eight (8)	
	Nine (9)	
	Ten (10)	
	Eleven (11)	
Dozen	*Twelve (12)*	

I showed the children the page in the book that introduces the word *several*. The photograph shows a girl with seven hats piled on her head and the text says, "If you have several hats, you have more than two or three." When we talked about *several* as being another word that doesn't refer to a specific number of things, Andrea had an insight: "*Several* is like the in-between of *few* and *many*. *Few* means a little. Then *several* means some, like more than a little but not a lot. And *many* means a whole bunch."

I thanked Andrea and asked the children to look at the Position chart. "Do you know what we could write after *third?*" I asked. This was easy for the children, and I listed the ordinal numbers up to twelfth, each with its corresponding numerical representation.

first (1st)	*seventh (7th)*
second (2d)	*eighth (8th)*
third (3d)	*ninth (9th)*
fourth (4th)	*tenth (10th)*
fifth (5th)	*eleventh (11th)*
sixth (6th)	*twelfth (12th)*

Without too much emphasis, I introduced the words *ordinal* and *cardinal*. I said, "These numbers on the Position chart are also called *ordinal* numbers because they tell us the *order* of things." I wrote *ordinal numbers* on the chart. "And numbers that tell us how many are called *cardinal* numbers." I wrote *cardinal numbers* on the How Many chart.

For the remaining time, the students worked in small table groups to come up with examples for each of the two charts. Each group had a recorder. After a while we came back together as a class to share ideas. Some of the examples that the students generated for the numbers on the Position chart were contests, bases on a baseball diamond, ballet positions, pages in a book, and the birth order of sisters and brothers. For the How Many chart, they thought of twins, triplets, only (referring to one), ton, ounces in a cup, and cans in a six-pack of soda.

The Wing on a Flea

In *The Wing on a Flea: A Book About Shapes* (2001), Ed Emberley presents the idea that geometric shapes can be found in the everyday world that surrounds us. Using brightly colored illustrations and simple rhymes, he introduces triangles, rectangles, and circles. The book helps kindergartners become familiar with the three shapes and their attributes and relate the shapes to the real world.

In this lesson, using the book as a model, kindergarten students use cutout triangles, rectangles, and circles to create their own look at the world around them.

MATERIALS

construction paper cutouts of triangles, rectangles, and circles, at least 1 of each shape per student (the shapes should vary from 1 to 3 inches)

3 sheets of chart paper, each with a sentence starter:

A triangle could be a _____.

A rectangle could be a _____.

A circle could be a _____.

sentence starter strips, 3 per student (see Blackline Masters)

9-by-12-inch black construction paper, 3 sheets per student

scraps of colorful construction paper, wallpaper, and wrapping paper

"Today I'd like to read you a book about shapes and where we can find them in our world," I told a class of kindergartners. The children grew excited when they saw the clown on the cover of *A Wing on a Flea.*

The book focuses first on a triangle, showing it as the wing on a flea, the beak on a bird, a bandit's bandana, an admiral's hat, the nose on a cat, the tip of a top, a tepee, and a tree. The focus then shifts to a rectangle, showing it as pieces of confetti, a bandage, a ruler, a pirate map, a box, blocks, and a tea bag. Finally the book shows a circle as a little green pea, eyes in the dark, a marble, a bubble, a ball, a balloon, wheels, the earth, the sun, the moon, and the hole in a key.

I read the book twice, the first time straight through without interruptions, and the second time asking students to come up and trace with a finger the geometric shapes in the illustrations. I explained that this week they would be creating their own book using shapes.

"I have one triangle, one rectangle, and one circle cutout for each of you," I told the children. "Your job is to imagine what your shapes could be. Today we'll work on the triangle page of our books."

I posted the sheet of chart paper on which I written the sentence starter about triangles and read, "A triangle could be a _____." Some children eagerly raised their hands, remembering what they saw in the book, while others looked perplexed. I called on those who had ideas and listed their thoughts on the chart paper.

Alexis started our list. "A triangle could be the nose on a cat," she said, patting her own nose. I wrote *nose* on the chart under the prompt, "A triangle could be _____ ."

I opened the book to the illustration that Alexis was referring to. "I see the cat's nose, and it is a triangle. I also see some other triangles in the picture," I said, encouraging the students to study it further. Eager hands went up. As students shared their ideas, I continued to record.

"I see a triangle in the basket the cat is sitting in," Dante said.

"Two triangles and a circle make the bow," added Savannah, referring to the bow on the handle of the basket.

"I see two more triangles, and they are the ears of the cat," Jordan said.

Having discussed all of the triangles on that particular page, I asked the children for more ways to complete our sentence: "A triangle could be . . . what else?"

Cece suggested, "A party hat, because they are pointy." She formed her hands into a triangle and put them on top of her head like a party hat.

"A piece of pizza," said Michaela.

Several more ideas were offered. Our list extended to include a bird's beak, a Christmas tree, a flag (the child meant a pendant), the top of a mountain, and a wing of a bird or flea.

I showed the students a piece of 9-by-12-inch black construction paper and a sentence strip with the same sentence starter as on the chart: "A triangle could be a _____." I asked Tony, one of the students who had not yet offered an idea, to tell what I should write in the blank.

"Witch's hat," he suggested. I carefully wrote his suggestion on the sentence strip and read the completed sentence aloud: "A triangle could be a witch's hat." I pasted the sentence strip at the bottom of the long side of the black construction paper, asking the children to watch closely as I modeled how much glue to put on the back of the strip.

Before letting the students get to work, I reviewed what they were to do, using as cues the picture magnets that we used regularly. "First, you need to think of an idea about what your triangle could be and decide what word to write on your sentence strip." I wrote *1* on the chalkboard and placed next to it a magnet that shows a lightbulb. The students were familiar with the lightbulb as a symbol for thinking of ideas or brainstorming, so this magnet would remind them that the first step was thinking.

I pointed to the blank line in the sentence starter. "Second, on the line on your sentence strip, complete the sentence by writing the letter sounds you hear in your word." I wrote *2* and, to remind them to write, placed next to it a magnet that shows a pencil.

"Third, glue your sentence strip to the bottom of the black paper the way I did," I said, holding up the black paper on which I had glued the example. I wrote *3*. To remind the children this step, I added a magnet that shows glue.

"What do you think the next step is?" I asked.

"Make our picture," the children chorused.

"You're right," I confirmed. I opened the book again and reread the pages that present the triangle. I explained how the children were to make their own illustrations: "Glue your triangle on the page, then add other shapes that you'll cut out of the very special paper I have for you to use." When I showed them the pile of scraps of construction paper, wallpaper, and wrapping paper I had amassed, "ohhs" rippled through the room, accompanied by a few "yeahs" and even some applause.

I gave a few further suggestions: "When we look at Mr. Emberley's artwork, do you see how he uses different papers to make his pictures more interesting?" I asked. The students nodded their heads. I continued, "So you should use a variety of paper, too. Use different types of paper in your illustration—construction paper, wallpaper, and wrapping paper." I held up an example of each type of paper.

"Do you have to use all three kinds?" Sara asked. "Because I just want to use the plain paper and the gold wrapping paper."

"Two kinds of paper would be fine," I said. "Using a variety of colors and types is what will make your picture interesting and fun to look at, just like the pictures in the book."

As the students watched, I walked to the work table at the back of the room where I had placed all the supplies they needed for the activity. The students sit in table groups and each group has a captain for the week. I said, "Would the captain of each group come back here to get the first piece of paper you'll need for this project?" Before giving the captains the sentence strips they needed for their group members, I said to the class, "Now you should do the first step. Think of something that a triangle could be and write it down. Then practice reading your sentence to someone else at your table group. When I come to visit your table, you will need to read your sentence to me, and then I will give you your black paper."

The captains took the sentence strips back to their teams and the students began to work. Some wrote a word down immediately. Others sat for a moment, then began to sound out a word and record the letters that matched the sounds. As I circulated, I helped some of the students spell their words by sounding out letters for them. They recorded the letter they thought matched each sound. As I checked with groups of students, I asked the team captain of that group to get one bottle of glue from the supply area for the table to share.

A few students couldn't come up with an idea. I rounded them up and led them to the chart we had generated earlier. I read through the list for "A triangle could be a _____." One student left with a smile on his face before I even finished reading. Another needed the choices narrowed down, so I picked two ideas and suggested that he pick one of them. The third child wanted to come up with an original idea that no one had thought of yet, so I suggested she walk around the classroom and look for triangles in unusual places. A few minutes later I spotted her diligently writing *book shelf*.

At this point in the lesson, I signaled the students to stop and look at me quietly. When all had complied, I said, "Boys and girls, I am very pleased how you've followed my directions so far. Listen carefully. When everyone at your table has glued their sentence to the bottom of their black paper, your captain needs to get the rest of the supplies for the project." I had put the remaining supplies in shoebox-size plastic tubs, one for each table group. Each tub contained enough cutout triangles so that each child could have one; a variety of scraps of construction paper, wallpaper, and wrapping paper; and a pair of scissors for each student.

I continued with the directions: "It's important that you plan your picture first before gluing anything down. First decide where your triangle will go and put it down on the black paper. Then cut out other shapes and place them on the black paper where you want them glued. Once you've planned your whole picture and all of the pieces on your black paper are exactly where you want them, raise your hand." I wanted to preview each child's artwork before they glued it to the black paper.

The captains delivered the supply tubs to their tables, and the children excitedly got to work describing what a triangle could be using cutout shapes. (See Figures 18–1 and 18–2.)

Figure 18–1: For Aboullah, a triangle could be a pizza slice.

A triangle could be a _peezefo Pizza with Cheese_

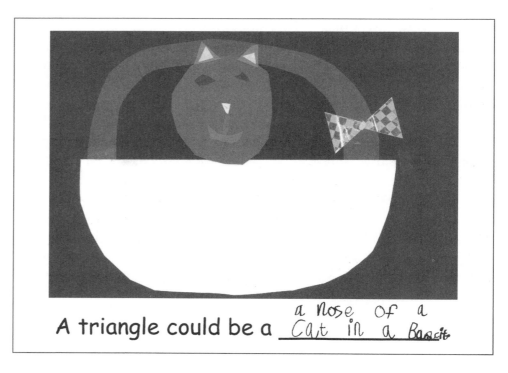

Figure 18–2: Amy found triangles in a cat's nose and ears, and in a bow.

A triangle could be a _a nose of a Cat in a Bascit_

On the next two days, we repeated the activity and the students completed pages for the rectangle (see Figures 18–3 and 18–4) and circle (see Figures 18–5 and 18–6) sentence prompts:

A rectangle could be a _____.
A circle could be a _____.

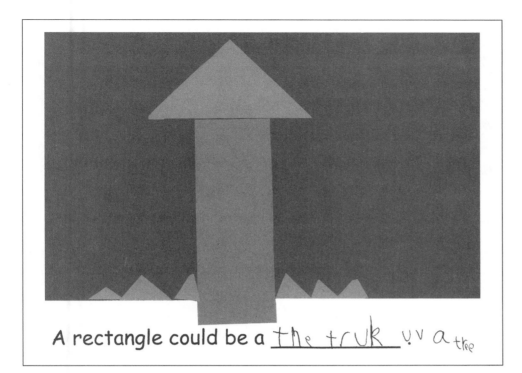

Figure 18–3: One student found a rectangle in the trunk of a tree.

A rectangle could be a _the truk_ v v a tree

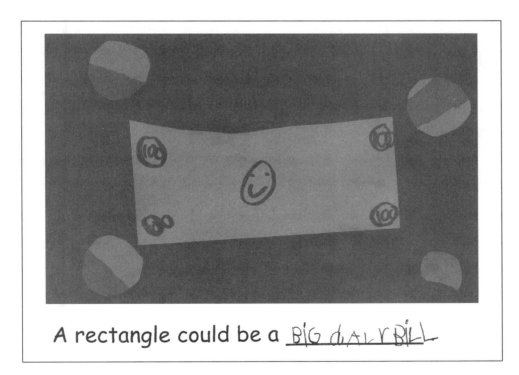

Figure 18–4: Tonny turned his rectangle into a "big dollar bill."

A rectangle could be a _BiG dALrBiLL_

To extend the lesson, I had each child make a clown, as Ed Emberley describes at the back of the book. For this activity the children need cutout shapes for the clown's face, eyes, nose, mouth, ears, and hat. I asked a parent volunteer to cut the shapes so that I had enough for every child.

Figure 18–5: For Conner, a circle was a roll of tape.

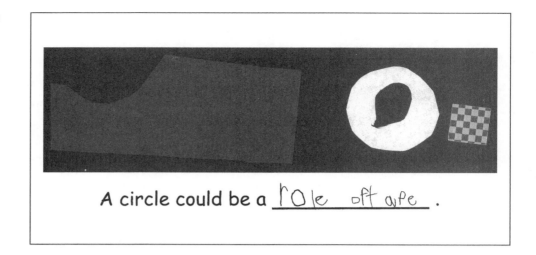

A circle could be a rOle oft ape .

Figure 18–6: Sam saw the moon as a circle.

A circle could be a MOON IN the. SCY

Blackline Masters

Animals Worksheet
1–100 Chart
Color Zoo Shapes
Measuring in the Classroom Worksheet
The Roman Numeral Game Rules
What Time Is It? Worksheet
The Wing on a Flea Sentence Starters

Animals

smaller than my hand . . .

larger than my hand . . .

1–100 Chart

1	2	3	4	5	6	7	8	9	10
11	12	13	14	15	16	17	18	19	20
21	22	23	24	25	26	27	28	29	30
31	32	33	34	35	36	37	38	39	40
41	42	43	44	45	46	47	48	49	50
51	52	53	54	55	56	57	58	59	60
61	62	63	64	65	66	67	68	69	70
71	72	73	74	75	76	77	78	79	80
81	82	83	84	85	86	87	88	89	90
91	92	93	94	95	96	97	98	99	100

From Math and Nonfiction, Grades K–2 by James Petersen. © 2004 Math Solutions Publications

star	heart
circle	oval
square	diamond
triangle	octagon
rectangle	hexagon

From *Math and Nonfiction, Grades K–2* by Jamee Petersen. © 2004 Math Solutions Publications

121

Measuring in the Classroom

Object	Span	Palm	Digit

From *Math and Nonfiction, Grades K–2* by Jamee Petersen. © 2004 Math Solutions Publications

The Roman Numeral Game Rules

You need:

- a partner
- a set of cards labeled 1 through 20 on one side and the equivalent Roman numerals on the opposite side:

1 = I	11 = XI
2 = II	12 = XII
3 = III	13 = XIII
4 = IV	14 = XIV
5 = V	15 = XV
6 = VI	16 = XVI
7 = VII	17 = XVII
8 = VIII	18 = XVIII
9 = IX	19 = IXX
10 = X	20 = XX

Rules

1. Spread all the cards out in front of both of you. It doesn't matter which side of a card is facing up.
2. Take turns. On your turn, point to a card, name the numeral on the other side, and then flip the card over to check. If you are correct, the card is yours. If you are not correct, leave the card in the center of the playing area.
3. After all cards have been collected, the winner is the player with the most number of cards.

Extension

Play the same way, but the winner is the player with the higher total value of his or her cards.

From *Math and Nonfiction, Grades K–2* by Jamee Petersen. © 2004 Math Solutions Publications

What Time Is It?

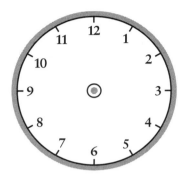

_____ : _____ _____

_____ : _____ _____

_____ : _____ _____

_____ : _____ _____

From *Math and Nonfiction, Grades K–2* by Jamee Petersen. ©2004 Math Solutions Publications

A triangle could be a _____ •

A rectangle could be a _____ •

A circle could be a _____ •

From *Math and Nonfiction, Grades K–2* by Jamee Petersen. © 2004 Math Solutions Publications

References

Adler, David A. 1999. *How Tall, How Short, How Faraway*. Illus. Nancy Tobin. New York: Holiday House.

Dotlich, Rebecca Kai. 1999. *What Is Square?* Photo. Maria Ferrari. New York: HarperFestival.

Ehlert, Lois. 1989. *Color Zoo*. New York: HarperFestival.

Emberley, Ed. 2001. *The Wing on a Flea: A Book About Shapes*. Boston: Little, Brown.

Fanelli, Sara. 1995. *My Map Book*. New York: HarperCollins.

Geisert, Arthur. 1996. *Roman Numerals I to MM: Numerabilia Romana Uno ad Duo Mila*. New York: Houghton Mifflin.

Hoban, Tana. 2000. *Cubes, Cones, Cylinders, and Spheres*. New York: Greenwillow Books.

Jenkins, Steve. 1995. *Biggest, Strongest, Fastest*. New York: Houghton Mifflin.

———. 1996. *Big and Little*. New York: Houghton Mifflin.

Johnson, Stephen T. 1998. *City by Numbers*. New York: Viking.

———. 1999. *Alphabet City*. New York: Puffin.

Older, Jules. 2001. *Telling Time: How to Tell Time on Digital and Analog Clocks!* Illus. Megan Halsey. Watertown, MA: Charlesbridge.

Rau, Dana Meachen. 2002. *A Star in My Orange: Looking for Nature's Shapes*. Brookfield, CT: Milbrook Press.

Schlein, Miriam. 1996. *More Than One*. Illus. Donald Crews. New York: Greenwillow Books.

Swinburne, Stephen. 2000. *What's a Pair? What's a Dozen?* Honesdale, PA: Boyds Mills Press.

St. George, Judith. 2000. *So You Want to Be President?* New York: Philomel Books.

Thornhill, Jan. 1997. *Before and After: A Book of Nature Timescapes.* Washington, DC: National Geographic Society.

Wells, Robert E. 2000. *Can You Count to a Googol?* Morton Grove, IL: Albert Whitman.

Williams, Rozanne Lanczak. 2001. *The Coin Counting Book.* Watertown, MA: Charlesbridge.